To:

From:

INSPO

~ Gift book

The best way to predict the future, is to create it.

~Abraham Lincoln

January. February. March. April. May. June. July. August. September. October. November. December.

Sunday. Monday. Tuesday. Wednesday. Thursday. Friday. Saturday

01|02|03|04|05|06|07|08|09|10|11|12|13|14|15|16|17|18|19|20|21|22|23|24|25|26|27|28|29|30

January. February. March. April. May. June. July. August. September. October. November. December.

Sunday. Monday. Tuesday. Wednesday. Thursday. Friday. Saturday

01|02|03|04|05|06|07|08|09|10|11|12|13|14|15|16|17|18|19|20|21|22|23|24|25|26|27|28|29|30

....

....

....

....

....

....

....

....

....

....

....

....

....

....

....

....

....

....

....

....

....

....

....

....

....

....

....

....

....

January. February. March. April. May. June. July. August. September. October. November. December.

Sunday. Monday. Tuesday. Wednesday. Thursday. Friday. Saturday

01|02|03|04|05|06|07|08|09|10|11|12|13|14|15|16|17|18|19|20|21|22|23|24|25|26|27|28|29|30

....

....

....

....

....

....

....

....

....

....

....

....

....

....

....

....

....

....

....

....

....

....

....

....

....

....

....

....

....

....

....

....

....

....

7

January. February. March. April. May. June. July. August. September. October. November. December.

Sunday. Monday. Tuesday. Wednesday. Thursday. Friday. Saturday

01|02|03|04|05|06|07|08|09|10|11|12|13|14|15|16|17|18|19|20|21|22|23|24|25|26|27|28|29|30

....

....

....

....

....

....

....

....

....

....

....

....

....

....

....

....

....

....

....

....

....

....

....

....

....

....

....

....

....

....

January. February. March. April. May. June. July. August. September. October. November. December.

Sunday. Monday. Tuesday. Wednesday. Thursday. Friday. Saturday

01|02|03|04|05|06|07|08|09|10|11|12|13|14|15|16|17|18|19|20|21|22|23|24|25|26|27|28|29|30

....

....

....

....

....

....

....

....

....

....

....

....

....

....

....

....

....

....

....

....

....

....

....

....

....

....

....

....

....

January.February.March.April.May.June.July.August.September.October.November.December.

Sunday.Monday.Tuesday.Wednesday.Thursday.Friday.Saturday

01|02|03|04|05|06|07|08|09|10|11|12|13|14|15|16|17|18|19|20|21|22|23|24|25|26|27|28|29|30

....
....
....
....
....
....
....
....
....
....
....
....
....
....
....
....
....
....
....
....
....
....
....
....
....
....
....
....
....
....

January.February.March.April.May.June.July.August.September.October.November.December.

Sunday.Monday.Tuesday.Wednesday.Thursday.Friday.Saturday

01|02|03|04|05|06|07|08|09|10|11|12|13|14|15|16|17|18|19|20|21|22|23|24|25|26|27|28|29|30

....
....
....
....
....
....
....
....
....
....
....
....
....
....
....
....
....
....
....
....
....
....
....
....
....
....
....
....
....
....

January. February. March. April. May. June. July. August. September. October. November. December.

Sunday. Monday. Tuesday. Wednesday. Thursday. Friday. Saturday

01|02|03|04|05|06|07|08|09|10|11|12|13|14|15|16|17|18|19|20|21|22|23|24|25|26|27|28|29|30

....

....

....

....

....

....

....

....

....

....

....

....

....

....

....

....

....

....

....

....

....

....

....

....

....

....

....

....

....

....

....

....

....

January. February. March. April. May. June. July. August. September. October. November. December.

Sunday. Monday. Tuesday. Wednesday. Thursday. Friday. Saturday

01|02|03|04|05|06|07|08|09|10|11|12|13|14|15|16|17|18|19|20|21|22|23|24|25|26|27|28|29|30

....

....

....

....

....

....

....

....

....

....

....

....

....

....

....

....

....

....

....

....

....

....

....

....

....

....

....

....

....

....

....

....

January. February. March. April. May. June. July. August. September. October. November. December.

Sunday. Monday. Tuesday. Wednesday. Thursday. Friday. Saturday

01|02|03|04|05|06|07|08|09|10|11|12|13|14|15|16|17|18|19|20|21|22|23|24|25|26|27|28|29|30

....

....

....

....

....

....

....

....

....

....

....

....

....

....

....

....

....

....

....

....

....

....

....

....

....

....

....

....

....

....

....

....

January. February. March. April. May. June. July. August. September. October. November. December.

Sunday. Monday. Tuesday. Wednesday. Thursday. Friday. Saturday

01|02|03|04|05|06|07|08|09|10|11|12|13|14|15|16|17|18|19|20|21|22|23|24|25|26|27|28|29|30

January. February. March. April. May. June. July. August. September. October. November. December.

Sunday. Monday. Tuesday. Wednesday. Thursday. Friday. Saturday

01|02|03|04|05|06|07|08|09|10|11|12|13|14|15|16|17|18|19|20|21|22|23|24|25|26|27|28|29|30

....

....

....

....

....

....

....

....

....

....

....

....

....

....

....

....

....

....

....

....

....

....

....

....

....

....

....

....

....

....

....

January. February. March. April. May. June. July. August. September. October. November. December.

Sunday. Monday. Tuesday. Wednesday. Thursday. Friday. Saturday

01|02|03|04|05|06|07|08|09|10|11|12|13|14|15|16|17|18|19|20|21|22|23|24|25|26|27|28|29|30

....
....
....
....
....
....
....
....
....
....
....
....
....
....
....
....
....
....
....
....
....
....
....
....
....
....
....
....
....
....

January. February. March. April. May. June. July. August. September. October. November. December.

Sunday. Monday. Tuesday. Wednesday. Thursday. Friday. Saturday

01|02|03|04|05|06|07|08|09|10|11|12|13|14|15|16|17|18|19|20|21|22|23|24|25|26|27|28|29|30

....

....

....

....

....

....

....

....

....

....

....

....

....

....

....

....

....

....

....

....

....

....

....

....

....

....

....

....

....

....

....

....

January. February. March. April. May. June. July. August. September. October. November. December.

Sunday. Monday. Tuesday. Wednesday. Thursday. Friday. Saturday

01|02|03|04|05|06|07|08|09|10|11|12|13|14|15|16|17|18|19|20|21|22|23|24|25|26|27|28|29|30

....

....

....

....

....

....

....

....

....

....

....

....

....

....

....

....

....

....

....

....

....

....

....

....

....

....

....

....

....

....

....

January. February. March. April. May. June. July. August. September. October. November. December.

Sunday. Monday. Tuesday. Wednesday. Thursday. Friday. Saturday

01|02|03|04|05|06|07|08|09|10|11|12|13|14|15|16|17|18|19|20|21|22|23|24|25|26|27|28|29|30

....
....
....
....
....
....
....
....
....
....
....
....
....
....
....
....
....
....
....
....
....
....
....
....
....
....
....
....
....
....

January. February. March. April. May. June. July. August. September. October. November. December.

Sunday. Monday. Tuesday. Wednesday. Thursday. Friday. Saturday

01|02|03|04|05|06|07|08|09|10|11|12|13|14|15|16|17|18|19|20|21|22|23|24|25|26|27|28|29|30

January.February.March.April.May.June.July.August.September.October.November.December.

Sunday.Monday.Tuesday.Wednesday.Thursday.Friday.Saturday

01|02|03|04|05|06|07|08|09|10|11|12|13|14|15|16|17|18|19|20|21|22|23|24|25|26|27|28|29|30

....
....
....
....
....
....
....
....
....
....
....
....
....
....
....
....
....
....
....
....
....
....
....
....
....
....
....
....
....
....
....
....
....
....

January. February. March. April. May. June. July. August. September. October. November. December.

Sunday. Monday. Tuesday. Wednesday. Thursday. Friday. Saturday

01|02|03|04|05|06|07|08|09|10|11|12|13|14|15|16|17|18|19|20|21|22|23|24|25|26|27|28|29|30

....
....
....
....
....
....
....
....
....
....
....
....
....
....
....
....
....
....
....
....
....
....
....
....
....
....
....
....
....
....
....
....
....
....
....
....

January. February. March. April. May. June. July. August. September. October. November. December.

Sunday. Monday. Tuesday. Wednesday. Thursday. Friday. Saturday

01|02|03|04|05|06|07|08|09|10|11|12|13|14|15|16|17|18|19|20|21|22|23|24|25|26|27|28|29|30

....

....

....

....

....

....

....

....

....

....

....

....

....

....

....

....

....

....

....

....

....

....

....

....

....

....

....

....

....

....

....

....

January. February. March. April. May. June. July. August. September. October. November. December.

Sunday. Monday. Tuesday. Wednesday. Thursday. Friday. Saturday

01|02|03|04|05|06|07|08|09|10|11|12|13|14|15|16|17|18|19|20|21|22|23|24|25|26|27|28|29|30

....
....
....
....
....
....
....
....
....
....
....
....
....
....
....
....
....
....
....
....
....
....
....
....
....
....
....
....
....
....

January. February. March. April. May. June. July. August. September. October. November. December.

Sunday. Monday. Tuesday. Wednesday. Thursday. Friday. Saturday

01|02|03|04|05|06|07|08|09|10|11|12|13|14|15|16|17|18|19|20|21|22|23|24|25|26|27|28|29|30

....

....

....

....

....

....

....

....

....

....

....

....

....

....

....

....

....

....

....

....

....

....

....

....

....

....

....

....

....

....

January. February. March. April. May. June. July. August. September. October. November. December.

Sunday. Monday. Tuesday. Wednesday. Thursday. Friday. Saturday

01|02|03|04|05|06|07|08|09|10|11|12|13|14|15|16|17|18|19|20|21|22|23|24|25|26|27|28|29|30

January. February. March. April. May. June. July. August. September. October. November. December.

Sunday. Monday. Tuesday. Wednesday. Thursday. Friday. Saturday

01|02|03|04|05|06|07|08|09|10|11|12|13|14|15|16|17|18|19|20|21|22|23|24|25|26|27|28|29|30

....

....

....

....

....

....

....

....

....

....

....

....

....

....

....

....

....

....

....

....

....

....

....

....

....

....

....

....

....

....

....

January. February. March. April. May. June. July. August. September. October. November. December.

Sunday. Monday. Tuesday. Wednesday. Thursday. Friday. Saturday

01|02|03|04|05|06|07|08|09|10|11|12|13|14|15|16|17|18|19|20|21|22|23|24|25|26|27|28|29|30

January. February. March. April. May. June. July. August. September. October. November. December.

Sunday. Monday. Tuesday. Wednesday. Thursday. Friday. Saturday

01|02|03|04|05|06|07|08|09|10|11|12|13|14|15|16|17|18|19|20|21|22|23|24|25|26|27|28|29|30

....

....

....

....

....

....

....

....

....

....

....

....

....

....

....

....

....

....

....

....

....

....

....

....

....

....

....

....

....

....

January. February. March. April. May. June. July. August. September. October. November. December.

Sunday. Monday. Tuesday. Wednesday. Thursday. Friday. Saturday

01|02|03|04|05|06|07|08|09|10|11|12|13|14|15|16|17|18|19|20|21|22|23|24|25|26|27|28|29|30

....
....
....
....
....
....
....
....
....
....
....
....
....
....
....
....
....
....
....
....
....
....
....
....
....
....
....
....
....
....
....

January. February. March. April. May. June. July. August. September. October. November. December.

Sunday. Monday. Tuesday. Wednesday. Thursday. Friday. Saturday

01|02|03|04|05|06|07|08|09|10|11|12|13|14|15|16|17|18|19|20|21|22|23|24|25|26|27|28|29|30

....

....

....

....

....

....

....

....

....

....

....

....

....

....

....

....

....

....

....

....

....

....

....

....

....

....

....

....

....

....

January. February. March. April. May. June. July. August. September. October. November. December.

Sunday. Monday. Tuesday. Wednesday. Thursday. Friday. Saturday

01|02|03|04|05|06|07|08|09|10|11|12|13|14|15|16|17|18|19|20|21|22|23|24|25|26|27|28|29|30

....
....
....
....
....
....
....
....
....
....
....
....
....
....
....
....
....
....
....
....
....
....
....
....
....
....
....
....
....
....
....
....
....
....

January. February. March. April. May. June. July. August. September. October. November. December.

Sunday. Monday. Tuesday. Wednesday. Thursday. Friday. Saturday

01|02|03|04|05|06|07|08|09|10|11|12|13|14|15|16|17|18|19|20|21|22|23|24|25|26|27|28|29|30

....
....
....
....
....
....
....
....
....
....
....
....
....
....
....
....
....
....
....
....
....
....
....
....
....
....
....
....
....
....
....

January. February. March. April. May. June. July. August. September. October. November. December.

Sunday. Monday. Tuesday. Wednesday. Thursday. Friday. Saturday

01|02|03|04|05|06|07|08|09|10|11|12|13|14|15|16|17|18|19|20|21|22|23|24|25|26|27|28|29|30

....

....

....

....

....

....

....

....

....

....

....

....

....

....

....

....

....

....

....

....

....

....

....

....

....

....

....

....

....

....

....

....

January. February. March. April. May. June. July. August. September. October. November. December.

Sunday. Monday. Tuesday. Wednesday. Thursday. Friday. Saturday

01|02|03|04|05|06|07|08|09|10|11|12|13|14|15|16|17|18|19|20|21|22|23|24|25|26|27|28|29|30

....

....

....

....

....

....

....

....

....

....

....

....

....

....

....

....

....

....

....

....

....

....

....

....

....

....

....

....

....

....

January. February. March. April. May. June. July. August. September. October. November. December.

Sunday. Monday. Tuesday. Wednesday. Thursday. Friday. Saturday

01|02|03|04|05|06|07|08|09|10|11|12|13|14|15|16|17|18|19|20|21|22|23|24|25|26|27|28|29|30

....

....

....

....

....

....

....

....

....

....

....

....

....

....

....

....

....

....

....

....

....

....

....

....

....

....

....

....

....

....

January. February. March. April. May. June. July. August. September. October. November. December.

Sunday. Monday. Tuesday. Wednesday. Thursday. Friday. Saturday

01|02|03|04|05|06|07|08|09|10|11|12|13|14|15|16|17|18|19|20|21|22|23|24|25|26|27|28|29|30

....

....

....

....

....

....

....

....

....

....

....

....

....

....

....

....

....

....

....

....

....

....

....

....

....

....

....

....

....

....

....

January. February. March. April. May. June. July. August. September. October. November. December.

Sunday. Monday. Tuesday. Wednesday. Thursday. Friday. Saturday

01|02|03|04|05|06|07|08|09|10|11|12|13|14|15|16|17|18|19|20|21|22|23|24|25|26|27|28|29|30

....
....
....
....
....
....
....
....
....
....
....
....
....
....
....
....
....
....
....
....
....
....
....
....
....
....
....
....
....
....
....
....
....

January. February. March. April. May. June. July. August. September. October. November. December.

Sunday. Monday. Tuesday. Wednesday. Thursday. Friday. Saturday

01|02|03|04|05|06|07|08|09|10|11|12|13|14|15|16|17|18|19|20|21|22|23|24|25|26|27|28|29|30

January. February. March. April. May. June. July. August. September. October. November. December.

Sunday. Monday. Tuesday. Wednesday. Thursday. Friday. Saturday

01|02|03|04|05|06|07|08|09|10|11|12|13|14|15|16|17|18|19|20|21|22|23|24|25|26|27|28|29|30

January. February. March. April. May. June. July. August. September. October. November. December.

Sunday. Monday. Tuesday. Wednesday. Thursday. Friday. Saturday

01|02|03|04|05|06|07|08|09|10|11|12|13|14|15|16|17|18|19|20|21|22|23|24|25|26|27|28|29|30

....

....

....

....

....

....

....

....

....

....

....

....

....

....

....

....

....

....

....

....

....

....

....

....

....

....

....

....

....

....

....

January. February. March. April. May. June. July. August. September. October. November. December.

Sunday. Monday. Tuesday. Wednesday. Thursday. Friday. Saturday

01|02|03|04|05|06|07|08|09|10|11|12|13|14|15|16|17|18|19|20|21|22|23|24|25|26|27|28|29|30

....

....

....

....

....

....

....

....

....

....

....

....

....

....

....

....

....

....

....

....

....

....

....

....

....

....

....

....

....

....

January.February.March.April.May.June.July.August.September.October.November.December.

Sunday.Monday.Tuesday.Wednesday.Thursday.Friday.Saturday

01|02|03|04|05|06|07|08|09|10|11|12|13|14|15|16|17|18|19|20|21|22|23|24|25|26|27|28|29|30

January. February. March. April. May. June. July. August. September. October. November. December.

Sunday. Monday. Tuesday. Wednesday. Thursday. Friday. Saturday

01|02|03|04|05|06|07|08|09|10|11|12|13|14|15|16|17|18|19|20|21|22|23|24|25|26|27|28|29|30

....
....
....
....
....
....
....
....
....
....
....
....
....
....
....
....
....
....
....
....
....
....
....
....
....
....
....
....
....
....
....
....
....

January. February. March. April. May. June. July. August. September. October. November. December.

Sunday. Monday. Tuesday. Wednesday. Thursday. Friday. Saturday

01|02|03|04|05|06|07|08|09|10|11|12|13|14|15|16|17|18|19|20|21|22|23|24|25|26|27|28|29|30

....

....

....

....

....

....

....

....

....

....

....

....

....

....

....

....

....

....

....

....

....

....

....

....

....

....

....

....

....

....

....

....

January. February. March. April. May. June. July. August. September. October. November. December.

Sunday. Monday. Tuesday. Wednesday. Thursday. Friday. Saturday

01|02|03|04|05|06|07|08|09|10|11|12|13|14|15|16|17|18|19|20|21|22|23|24|25|26|27|28|29|30

January. February. March. April. May. June. July. August. September. October. November. December.

Sunday. Monday. Tuesday. Wednesday. Thursday. Friday. Saturday

01|02|03|04|05|06|07|08|09|10|11|12|13|14|15|16|17|18|19|20|21|22|23|24|25|26|27|28|29|30

....

....

....

....

....

....

....

....

....

....

....

....

....

....

....

....

....

....

....

....

....

....

....

....

....

....

....

....

....

....

....

January. February. March. April. May. June. July. August. September. October. November. December.

Sunday. Monday. Tuesday. Wednesday. Thursday. Friday. Saturday

01|02|03|04|05|06|07|08|09|10|11|12|13|14|15|16|17|18|19|20|21|22|23|24|25|26|27|28|29|30

....

....

....

....

....

....

....

....

....

....

....

....

....

....

....

....

....

....

....

....

....

....

....

....

....

....

....

....

....

....

....

....

....

January. February. March. April. May. June. July. August. September. October. November. December.

Sunday. Monday. Tuesday. Wednesday. Thursday. Friday. Saturday

01|02|03|04|05|06|07|08|09|10|11|12|13|14|15|16|17|18|19|20|21|22|23|24|25|26|27|28|29|30

....

....

....

....

....

....

....

....

....

....

....

....

....

....

....

....

....

....

....

....

....

....

....

....

....

....

....

....

....

....

January. February. March. April. May. June. July. August. September. October. November. December.

Sunday. Monday. Tuesday. Wednesday. Thursday. Friday. Saturday

01|02|03|04|05|06|07|08|09|10|11|12|13|14|15|16|17|18|19|20|21|22|23|24|25|26|27|28|29|30

....

....

....

....

....

....

....

....

....

....

....

....

....

....

....

....

....

....

....

....

....

....

....

....

....

....

....

....

....

....

....

....

January. February. March. April. May. June. July. August. September. October. November. December.

Sunday. Monday. Tuesday. Wednesday. Thursday. Friday. Saturday

01|02|03|04|05|06|07|08|09|10|11|12|13|14|15|16|17|18|19|20|21|22|23|24|25|26|27|28|29|30

....

....

....

....

....

....

....

....

....

....

....

....

....

....

....

....

....

....

....

....

....

....

....

....

....

....

....

....

....

....

....

....

....

January. February. March. April. May. June. July. August. September. October. November. December.

Sunday. Monday. Tuesday. Wednesday. Thursday. Friday. Saturday

01|02|03|04|05|06|07|08|09|10|11|12|13|14|15|16|17|18|19|20|21|22|23|24|25|26|27|28|29|30

January. February. March. April. May. June. July. August. September. October. November. December.

Sunday. Monday. Tuesday. Wednesday. Thursday. Friday. Saturday

01|02|03|04|05|06|07|08|09|10|11|12|13|14|15|16|17|18|19|20|21|22|23|24|25|26|27|28|29|30

....
....
....
....
....
....
....
....
....
....
....
....
....
....
....
....
....
....
....
....
....
....
....
....
....
....
....
....
....
....
....

January. February. March. April. May. June. July. August. September. October. November. December.

Sunday. Monday. Tuesday. Wednesday. Thursday. Friday. Saturday

01|02|03|04|05|06|07|08|09|10|11|12|13|14|15|16|17|18|19|20|21|22|23|24|25|26|27|28|29|30

....

....

....

....

....

....

....

....

....

....

....

....

....

....

....

....

....

....

....

....

....

....

....

....

....

....

....

....

....

....

January. February. March. April. May. June. July. August. September. October. November. December.

Sunday. Monday. Tuesday. Wednesday. Thursday. Friday. Saturday

01|02|03|04|05|06|07|08|09|10|11|12|13|14|15|16|17|18|19|20|21|22|23|24|25|26|27|28|29|30

....

....

....

....

....

....

....

....

....

....

....

....

....

....

....

....

....

....

....

....

....

....

....

....

....

....

....

....

....

....

....

....

January. February. March. April. May. June. July. August. September. October. November. December.

Sunday. Monday. Tuesday. Wednesday. Thursday. Friday. Saturday

01|02|03|04|05|06|07|08|09|10|11|12|13|14|15|16|17|18|19|20|21|22|23|24|25|26|27|28|29|30

....

....

....

....

....

....

....

....

....

....

....

....

....

....

....

....

....

....

....

....

....

....

....

....

....

....

....

....

....

....

....

....

....

January. February. March. April. May. June. July. August. September. October. November. December.

Sunday. Monday. Tuesday. Wednesday. Thursday. Friday. Saturday

01|02|03|04|05|06|07|08|09|10|11|12|13|14|15|16|17|18|19|20|21|22|23|24|25|26|27|28|29|30

....

....

....

....

....

....

....

....

....

....

....

....

....

....

....

....

....

....

....

....

....

....

....

....

....

....

....

....

....

....

January. February. March. April. May. June. July. August. September. October. November. December.

Sunday. Monday. Tuesday. Wednesday. Thursday. Friday. Saturday

01|02|03|04|05|06|07|08|09|10|11|12|13|14|15|16|17|18|19|20|21|22|23|24|25|26|27|28|29|30

January. February. March. April. May. June. July. August. September. October. November. December.

Sunday. Monday. Tuesday. Wednesday. Thursday. Friday. Saturday

01|02|03|04|05|06|07|08|09|10|11|12|13|14|15|16|17|18|19|20|21|22|23|24|25|26|27|28|29|30

January. February. March. April. May. June. July. August. September. October. November. December.

Sunday. Monday. Tuesday. Wednesday. Thursday. Friday. Saturday

01|02|03|04|05|06|07|08|09|10|11|12|13|14|15|16|17|18|19|20|21|22|23|24|25|26|27|28|29|30

....

....

....

....

....

....

....

....

....

....

....

....

....

....

....

....

....

....

....

....

....

....

....

....

....

....

....

....

....

....

....

....

....

January. February. March. April. May. June. July. August. September. October. November. December.

Sunday. Monday. Tuesday. Wednesday. Thursday. Friday. Saturday

01|02|03|04|05|06|07|08|09|10|11|12|13|14|15|16|17|18|19|20|21|22|23|24|25|26|27|28|29|30

....

....

....

....

....

....

....

....

....

....

....

....

....

....

....

....

....

....

....

....

....

....

....

....

....

....

....

....

....

....

....

....

....

January. February. March. April. May. June. July. August. September. October. November. December.

Sunday. Monday. Tuesday. Wednesday. Thursday. Friday. Saturday

01|02|03|04|05|06|07|08|09|10|11|12|13|14|15|16|17|18|19|20|21|22|23|24|25|26|27|28|29|30

....
....
....
....
....
....
....
....
....
....
....
....
....
....
....
....
....
....
....
....
....
....
....
....
....
....
....
....
....
....
....

January. February. March. April. May. June. July. August. September. October. November. December.

Sunday. Monday. Tuesday. Wednesday. Thursday. Friday. Saturday

01|02|03|04|05|06|07|08|09|10|11|12|13|14|15|16|17|18|19|20|21|22|23|24|25|26|27|28|29|30

....
....
....
....
....
....
....
....
....
....
....
....
....
....
....
....
....
....
....
....
....
....
....
....
....
....
....
....
....
....
....
....

January. February. March. April. May. June. July. August. September. October. November. December.

Sunday. Monday. Tuesday. Wednesday. Thursday. Friday. Saturday

01|02|03|04|05|06|07|08|09|10|11|12|13|14|15|16|17|18|19|20|21|22|23|24|25|26|27|28|29|30

....
....
....
....
....
....
....
....
....
....
....
....
....
....
....
....
....
....
....
....
....
....
....
....
....
....
....
....
....
....

January. February. March. April. May. June. July. August. September. October. November. December.

Sunday. Monday. Tuesday. Wednesday. Thursday. Friday. Saturday

01|02|03|04|05|06|07|08|09|10|11|12|13|14|15|16|17|18|19|20|21|22|23|24|25|26|27|28|29|30

....
....
....
....
....
....
....
....
....
....
....
....
....
....
....
....
....
....
....
....
....
....
....
....
....
....
....
....
....
....

January. February. March. April. May. June. July. August. September. October. November. December.

Sunday. Monday. Tuesday. Wednesday. Thursday. Friday. Saturday

01|02|03|04|05|06|07|08|09|10|11|12|13|14|15|16|17|18|19|20|21|22|23|24|25|26|27|28|29|30

January. February. March. April. May. June. July. August. September. October. November. December.

Sunday. Monday. Tuesday. Wednesday. Thursday. Friday. Saturday

01|02|03|04|05|06|07|08|09|10|11|12|13|14|15|16|17|18|19|20|21|22|23|24|25|26|27|28|29|30

....

....

....

....

....

....

....

....

....

....

....

....

....

....

....

....

....

....

....

....

....

....

....

....

....

....

....

....

....

....

January, February, March, April, May, June, July, August, September, October, November, December.

Sunday, Monday, Tuesday, Wednesday, Thursday, Friday, Saturday

01|02|03|04|05|06|07|08|09|10|11|12|13|14|15|16|17|18|19|20|21|22|23|24|25|26|27|28|29|30

....

....

....

....

....

....

....

....

....

....

....

....

....

....

....

....

....

....

....

....

....

....

....

....

....

....

....

....

....

....

....

....

....

....

....

January. February. March. April. May. June. July. August. September. October. November. December.

Sunday. Monday. Tuesday. Wednesday. Thursday. Friday. Saturday

01|02|03|04|05|06|07|08|09|10|11|12|13|14|15|16|17|18|19|20|21|22|23|24|25|26|27|28|29|30

January.February.March.April.May.June.July.August.September.October.November.December.

Sunday.Monday.Tuesday.Wednesday.Thursday.Friday.Saturday

01|02|03|04|05|06|07|08|09|10|11|12|13|14|15|16|17|18|19|20|21|22|23|24|25|26|27|28|29|30

January. February. March. April. May. June. July. August. September. October. November. December.

Sunday. Monday. Tuesday. Wednesday. Thursday. Friday. Saturday

01|02|03|04|05|06|07|08|09|10|11|12|13|14|15|16|17|18|19|20|21|22|23|24|25|26|27|28|29|30

....

....

....

....

....

....

....

....

....

....

....

....

....

....

....

....

....

....

....

....

....

....

....

....

....

....

....

....

....

....

....

January. February. March. April. May. June. July. August. September. October. November. December.

Sunday. Monday. Tuesday. Wednesday. Thursday. Friday. Saturday

01|02|03|04|05|06|07|08|09|10|11|12|13|14|15|16|17|18|19|20|21|22|23|24|25|26|27|28|29|30

....
....
....
....
....
....
....
....
....
....
....
....
....
....
....
....
....
....
....
....
....
....
....
....
....
....
....
....
....
....

January. February. March. April. May. June. July. August. September. October. November. December.

Sunday. Monday. Tuesday. Wednesday. Thursday. Friday. Saturday

01|02|03|04|05|06|07|08|09|10|11|12|13|14|15|16|17|18|19|20|21|22|23|24|25|26|27|28|29|30

January. February. March. April. May. June. July. August. September. October. November. December.

Sunday. Monday. Tuesday. Wednesday. Thursday. Friday. Saturday

01|02|03|04|05|06|07|08|09|10|11|12|13|14|15|16|17|18|19|20|21|22|23|24|25|26|27|28|29|30

January.February.March.April.May.June.July.August.September.October.November.December.

Sunday.Monday.Tuesday.Wednesday.Thursday.Friday.Saturday

01|02|03|04|05|06|07|08|09|10|11|12|13|14|15|16|17|18|19|20|21|22|23|24|25|26|27|28|29|30

....
....
....
....
....
....
....
....
....
....
....
....
....
....
....
....
....
....
....
....
....
....
....
....
....
....
....
....
....
....
....
....

January. February. March. April. May. June. July. August. September. October. November. December.

Sunday. Monday. Tuesday. Wednesday. Thursday. Friday. Saturday

01|02|03|04|05|06|07|08|09|10|11|12|13|14|15|16|17|18|19|20|21|22|23|24|25|26|27|28|29|30

January.February.March.April.May.June.July.August.September.October.November.December.

Sunday.Monday.Tuesday.Wednesday.Thursday.Friday.Saturday

01|02|03|04|05|06|07|08|09|10|11|12|13|14|15|16|17|18|19|20|21|22|23|24|25|26|27|28|29|30

January. February. March. April. May. June. July. August. September. October. November. December.

Sunday. Monday. Tuesday. Wednesday. Thursday. Friday. Saturday

01|02|03|04|05|06|07|08|09|10|11|12|13|14|15|16|17|18|19|20|21|22|23|24|25|26|27|28|29|30

January. February. March. April. May. June. July. August. September. October. November. December.

Sunday. Monday. Tuesday. Wednesday. Thursday. Friday. Saturday

01|02|03|04|05|06|07|08|09|10|11|12|13|14|15|16|17|18|19|20|21|22|23|24|25|26|27|28|29|30

....
....
....
....
....
....
....
....
....
....
....
....
....
....
....
....
....
....
....
....
....
....
....
....
....
....
....
....
....
....
....
....

January. February. March. April. May. June. July. August. September. October. November. December.

Sunday. Monday. Tuesday. Wednesday. Thursday. Friday. Saturday

01|02|03|04|05|06|07|08|09|10|11|12|13|14|15|16|17|18|19|20|21|22|23|24|25|26|27|28|29|30

....

....

....

....

....

....

....

....

....

....

....

....

....

....

....

....

....

....

....

....

....

....

....

....

....

....

....

....

....

....

....

....

....

....

....

....

January.February.March.April.May.June.July.August.September.October.November.December.

Sunday.Monday.Tuesday.Wednesday.Thursday.Friday.Saturday

01|02|03|04|05|06|07|08|09|10|11|12|13|14|15|16|17|18|19|20|21|22|23|24|25|26|27|28|29|30

....

....

....

....

....

....

....

....

....

....

....

....

....

....

....

....

....

....

....

....

....

....

....

....

....

....

....

....

....

....

January. February. March. April. May. June. July. August. September. October. November. December.

Sunday. Monday. Tuesday. Wednesday. Thursday. Friday. Saturday

01|02|03|04|05|06|07|08|09|10|11|12|13|14|15|16|17|18|19|20|21|22|23|24|25|26|27|28|29|30

January. February. March. April. May. June. July. August. September. October. November. December.

Sunday. Monday. Tuesday. Wednesday. Thursday. Friday. Saturday

01|02|03|04|05|06|07|08|09|10|11|12|13|14|15|16|17|18|19|20|21|22|23|24|25|26|27|28|29|30

....
....
....
....
....
....
....
....
....
....
....
....
....
....
....
....
....
....
....
....
....
....
....
....
....
....
....
....
....
....
....

January. February. March. April. May. June. July. August. September. October. November. December.

Sunday. Monday. Tuesday. Wednesday. Thursday. Friday. Saturday

01|02|03|04|05|06|07|08|09|10|11|12|13|14|15|16|17|18|19|20|21|22|23|24|25|26|27|28|29|30

....

....

....

....

....

....

....

....

....

....

....

....

....

....

....

....

....

....

....

....

....

....

....

....

....

....

....

....

....

....

January. February. March. April. May. June. July. August. September. October. November. December.

Sunday. Monday. Tuesday. Wednesday. Thursday. Friday. Saturday

01|02|03|04|05|06|07|08|09|10|11|12|13|14|15|16|17|18|19|20|21|22|23|24|25|26|27|28|29|30

January. February. March. April. May. June. July. August. September. October. November. December.

Sunday. Monday. Tuesday. Wednesday. Thursday. Friday. Saturday

01|02|03|04|05|06|07|08|09|10|11|12|13|14|15|16|17|18|19|20|21|22|23|24|25|26|27|28|29|30

....
....
....
....
....
....
....
....
....
....
....
....
....
....
....
....
....
....
....
....
....
....
....
....
....
....
....
....
....
....
....

January. February. March. April. May. June. July. August. September. October. November. December.

Sunday. Monday. Tuesday. Wednesday. Thursday. Friday. Saturday

01|02|03|04|05|06|07|08|09|10|11|12|13|14|15|16|17|18|19|20|21|22|23|24|25|26|27|28|29|30

....

....

....

....

....

....

....

....

....

....

....

....

....

....

....

....

....

....

....

....

....

....

....

....

....

....

....

....

....

....

....

....

January. February. March. April. May. June. July. August. September. October. November. December.

Sunday. Monday. Tuesday. Wednesday. Thursday. Friday. Saturday

01|02|03|04|05|06|07|08|09|10|11|12|13|14|15|16|17|18|19|20|21|22|23|24|25|26|27|28|29|30

January. February. March. April. May. June. July. August. September. October. November. December.

Sunday. Monday. Tuesday. Wednesday. Thursday. Friday. Saturday

01|02|03|04|05|06|07|08|09|10|11|12|13|14|15|16|17|18|19|20|21|22|23|24|25|26|27|28|29|30

January. February. March. April. May. June. July. August. September. October. November. December.

Sunday. Monday. Tuesday. Wednesday. Thursday. Friday. Saturday

01|02|03|04|05|06|07|08|09|10|11|12|13|14|15|16|17|18|19|20|21|22|23|24|25|26|27|28|29|30

January. February. March. April. May. June. July. August. September. October. November. December.

Sunday. Monday. Tuesday. Wednesday. Thursday. Friday. Saturday

01|02|03|04|05|06|07|08|09|10|11|12|13|14|15|16|17|18|19|20|21|22|23|24|25|26|27|28|29|30

....
....
....
....
....
....
....
....
....
....
....
....
....
....
....
....
....
....
....
....
....
....
....
....
....
....
....
....
....
....

January. February. March. April. May. June. July. August. September. October. November. December.

Sunday. Monday. Tuesday. Wednesday. Thursday. Friday. Saturday

01|02|03|04|05|06|07|08|09|10|11|12|13|14|15|16|17|18|19|20|21|22|23|24|25|26|27|28|29|30

....

....

....

....

....

....

....

....

....

....

....

....

....

....

....

....

....

....

....

....

....

....

....

....

....

....

....

....

....

....

....

....

January. February. March. April. May. June. July. August. September. October. November. December.

Sunday. Monday. Tuesday. Wednesday. Thursday. Friday. Saturday

01|02|03|04|05|06|07|08|09|10|11|12|13|14|15|16|17|18|19|20|21|22|23|24|25|26|27|28|29|30

January. February. March. April. May. June. July. August. September. October. November. December.

Sunday. Monday. Tuesday. Wednesday. Thursday. Friday. Saturday

01|02|03|04|05|06|07|08|09|10|11|12|13|14|15|16|17|18|19|20|21|22|23|24|25|26|27|28|29|30

January. February. March. April. May. June. July. August. September. October. November. December.

Sunday. Monday. Tuesday. Wednesday. Thursday. Friday. Saturday

01|02|03|04|05|06|07|08|09|10|11|12|13|14|15|16|17|18|19|20|21|22|23|24|25|26|27|28|29|30

January. February. March. April. May. June. July. August. September. October. November. December.

Sunday. Monday. Tuesday. Wednesday. Thursday. Friday. Saturday

01|02|03|04|05|06|07|08|09|10|11|12|13|14|15|16|17|18|19|20|21|22|23|24|25|26|27|28|29|30

January. February. March. April. May. June. July. August. September. October. November. December.

Sunday. Monday. Tuesday. Wednesday. Thursday. Friday. Saturday

01|02|03|04|05|06|07|08|09|10|11|12|13|14|15|16|17|18|19|20|21|22|23|24|25|26|27|28|29|30

....
....
....
....
....
....
....
....
....
....
....
....
....
....
....
....
....
....
....
....
....
....
....
....
....
....
....
....
....
....
....
....

January. February. March. April. May. June. July. August. September. October. November. December.

Sunday. Monday. Tuesday. Wednesday. Thursday. Friday. Saturday

01|02|03|04|05|06|07|08|09|10|11|12|13|14|15|16|17|18|19|20|21|22|23|24|25|26|27|28|29|30

January. February. March. April. May. June. July. August. September. October. November. December.

Sunday. Monday. Tuesday. Wednesday. Thursday. Friday. Saturday

01|02|03|04|05|06|07|08|09|10|11|12|13|14|15|16|17|18|19|20|21|22|23|24|25|26|27|28|29|30

....

....

....

....

....

....

....

....

....

....

....

....

....

....

....

....

....

....

....

....

....

....

....

....

....

....

....

....

....

....

....

January. February. March. April. May. June. July. August. September. October. November. December.

Sunday. Monday. Tuesday. Wednesday. Thursday. Friday. Saturday

01|02|03|04|05|06|07|08|09|10|11|12|13|14|15|16|17|18|19|20|21|22|23|24|25|26|27|28|29|30

January. February. March. April. May. June. July. August. September. October. November. December.

Sunday. Monday. Tuesday. Wednesday. Thursday. Friday. Saturday

01|02|03|04|05|06|07|08|09|10|11|12|13|14|15|16|17|18|19|20|21|22|23|24|25|26|27|28|29|30

January. February. March. April. May. June. July. August. September. October. November. December.

Sunday. Monday. Tuesday. Wednesday. Thursday. Friday. Saturday

01|02|03|04|05|06|07|08|09|10|11|12|13|14|15|16|17|18|19|20|21|22|23|24|25|26|27|28|29|30

January. February. March. April. May. June. July. August. September. October. November. December.

Sunday. Monday. Tuesday. Wednesday. Thursday. Friday. Saturday

01|02|03|04|05|06|07|08|09|10|11|12|13|14|15|16|17|18|19|20|21|22|23|24|25|26|27|28|29|30

....

....

....

....

....

....

....

....

....

....

....

....

....

....

....

....

....

....

....

....

....

....

....

....

....

....

....

....

....

....

January. February. March. April. May. June. July. August. September. October. November. December.

Sunday. Monday. Tuesday. Wednesday. Thursday. Friday. Saturday

01|02|03|04|05|06|07|08|09|10|11|12|13|14|15|16|17|18|19|20|21|22|23|24|25|26|27|28|29|30

....

....

....

....

....

....

....

....

....

....

....

....

....

....

....

....

....

....

....

....

....

....

....

....

....

....

....

....

....

....

....

....

....

....

....

....

....

January.February.March.April.May.June.July.August.September.October.November.December.

Sunday.Monday.Tuesday.Wednesday.Thursday.Friday.Saturday

01|02|03|04|05|06|07|08|09|10|11|12|13|14|15|16|17|18|19|20|21|22|23|24|25|26|27|28|29|30

January. February. March. April. May. June. July. August. September. October. November. December.

Sunday. Monday. Tuesday. Wednesday. Thursday. Friday. Saturday

01|02|03|04|05|06|07|08|09|10|11|12|13|14|15|16|17|18|19|20|21|22|23|24|25|26|27|28|29|30

January. February. March. April. May. June. July. August. September. October. November. December.

Sunday. Monday. Tuesday. Wednesday. Thursday. Friday. Saturday

01|02|03|04|05|06|07|08|09|10|11|12|13|14|15|16|17|18|19|20|21|22|23|24|25|26|27|28|29|30

January.February.March.April.May.June.July.August.September.October.November.December.

Sunday.Monday.Tuesday.Wednesday.Thursday.Friday.Saturday

01|02|03|04|05|06|07|08|09|10|11|12|13|14|15|16|17|18|19|20|21|22|23|24|25|26|27|28|29|30

January. February. March. April. May. June. July. August. September. October. November. December.

Sunday. Monday. Tuesday. Wednesday. Thursday. Friday. Saturday

01|02|03|04|05|06|07|08|09|10|11|12|13|14|15|16|17|18|19|20|21|22|23|24|25|26|27|28|29|30

January. February. March. April. May. June. July. August. September. October. November. December.

Sunday. Monday. Tuesday. Wednesday. Thursday. Friday. Saturday

01|02|03|04|05|06|07|08|09|10|11|12|13|14|15|16|17|18|19|20|21|22|23|24|25|26|27|28|29|30

January. February. March. April. May. June. July. August. September. October. November. December.

Sunday. Monday. Tuesday. Wednesday. Thursday. Friday. Saturday

01|02|03|04|05|06|07|08|09|10|11|12|13|14|15|16|17|18|19|20|21|22|23|24|25|26|27|28|29|30

....

....

....

....

....

....

....

....

....

....

....

....

....

....

....

....

....

....

....

....

....

....

....

....

....

....

....

....

....

January. February. March. April. May. June. July. August. September. October. November. December.

Sunday. Monday. Tuesday. Wednesday. Thursday. Friday. Saturday

01|02|03|04|05|06|07|08|09|10|11|12|13|14|15|16|17|18|19|20|21|22|23|24|25|26|27|28|29|30

January. February. March. April. May. June. July. August. September. October. November. December.

Sunday. Monday. Tuesday. Wednesday. Thursday. Friday. Saturday

01|02|03|04|05|06|07|08|09|10|11|12|13|14|15|16|17|18|19|20|21|22|23|24|25|26|27|28|29|30

....

....

....

....

....

....

....

....

....

....

....

....

....

....

....

....

....

....

....

....

....

....

....

....

....

....

....

....

....

....

....

....

....

....

....

January. February. March. April. May. June. July. August. September. October. November. December.

Sunday. Monday. Tuesday. Wednesday. Thursday. Friday. Saturday

01|02|03|04|05|06|07|08|09|10|11|12|13|14|15|16|17|18|19|20|21|22|23|24|25|26|27|28|29|30

January. February. March. April. May. June. July. August. September. October. November. December.

Sunday. Monday. Tuesday. Wednesday. Thursday. Friday. Saturday

01|02|03|04|05|06|07|08|09|10|11|12|13|14|15|16|17|18|19|20|21|22|23|24|25|26|27|28|29|30

January. February. March. April. May. June. July. August. September. October. November. December.

Sunday. Monday. Tuesday. Wednesday. Thursday. Friday. Saturday

01|02|03|04|05|06|07|08|09|10|11|12|13|14|15|16|17|18|19|20|21|22|23|24|25|26|27|28|29|30

January. February. March. April. May. June. July. August. September. October. November. December.

Sunday. Monday. Tuesday. Wednesday. Thursday. Friday. Saturday

01|02|03|04|05|06|07|08|09|10|11|12|13|14|15|16|17|18|19|20|21|22|23|24|25|26|27|28|29|30

....
....
....
....
....
....
....
....
....
....
....
....
....
....
....
....
....
....
....
....
....
....
....
....
....
....
....
....
....
....
....

January. February. March. April. May. June. July. August. September. October. November. December.

Sunday. Monday. Tuesday. Wednesday. Thursday. Friday. Saturday

01|02|03|04|05|06|07|08|09|10|11|12|13|14|15|16|17|18|19|20|21|22|23|24|25|26|27|28|29|30

119

January. February. March. April. May. June. July. August. September. October. November. December.

Sunday. Monday. Tuesday. Wednesday. Thursday. Friday. Saturday

01|02|03|04|05|06|07|08|09|10|11|12|13|14|15|16|17|18|19|20|21|22|23|24|25|26|27|28|29|30

January. February. March. April. May. June. July. August. September. October. November. December.

Sunday. Monday. Tuesday. Wednesday. Thursday. Friday. Saturday

01|02|03|04|05|06|07|08|09|10|11|12|13|14|15|16|17|18|19|20|21|22|23|24|25|26|27|28|29|30

....

....

....

....

....

....

....

....

....

....

....

....

....

....

....

....

....

....

....

....

....

....

....

....

....

....

....

....

....

....

....

....

....

January. February. March. April. May. June. July. August. September. October. November. December.

Sunday. Monday. Tuesday. Wednesday. Thursday. Friday. Saturday

01|02|03|04|05|06|07|08|09|10|11|12|13|14|15|16|17|18|19|20|21|22|23|24|25|26|27|28|29|30

January. February. March. April. May. June. July. August. September. October. November. December.

Sunday. Monday. Tuesday. Wednesday. Thursday. Friday. Saturday

01|02|03|04|05|06|07|08|09|10|11|12|13|14|15|16|17|18|19|20|21|22|23|24|25|26|27|28|29|30

January. February. March. April. May. June. July. August. September. October. November. December.

Sunday. Monday. Tuesday. Wednesday. Thursday. Friday. Saturday

01|02|03|04|05|06|07|08|09|10|11|12|13|14|15|16|17|18|19|20|21|22|23|24|25|26|27|28|29|30

....
....
....
....
....
....
....
....
....
....
....
....
....
....
....
....
....
....
....
....
....
....
....
....
....
....
....
....
....
....
....

January. February. March. April. May. June. July. August. September. October. November. December.

Sunday. Monday. Tuesday. Wednesday. Thursday. Friday. Saturday

01|02|03|04|05|06|07|08|09|10|11|12|13|14|15|16|17|18|19|20|21|22|23|24|25|26|27|28|29|30

....

....

....

....

....

....

....

....

....

....

....

....

....

....

....

....

....

....

....

....

....

....

....

....

....

....

....

....

....

....

....

....

....

January. February. March. April. May. June. July. August. September. October. November. December.

Sunday. Monday. Tuesday. Wednesday. Thursday. Friday. Saturday

01|02|03|04|05|06|07|08|09|10|11|12|13|14|15|16|17|18|19|20|21|22|23|24|25|26|27|28|29|30

January, February, March, April, May, June, July, August, September, October, November, December.

Sunday, Monday, Tuesday, Wednesday, Thursday, Friday, Saturday

01|02|03|04|05|06|07|08|09|10|11|12|13|14|15|16|17|18|19|20|21|22|23|24|25|26|27|28|29|30

January. February. March. April. May. June. July. August. September. October. November. December.

Sunday. Monday. Tuesday. Wednesday. Thursday. Friday. Saturday

01|02|03|04|05|06|07|08|09|10|11|12|13|14|15|16|17|18|19|20|21|22|23|24|25|26|27|28|29|30

....

....

....

....

....

....

....

....

....

....

....

....

....

....

....

....

....

....

....

....

....

....

....

....

....

....

....

....

....

....

....

January. February. March. April. May. June. July. August. September. October. November. December.

Sunday. Monday. Tuesday. Wednesday. Thursday. Friday. Saturday

01|02|03|04|05|06|07|08|09|10|11|12|13|14|15|16|17|18|19|20|21|22|23|24|25|26|27|28|29|30

January.February.March.April.May.June.July.August.September.October.November.December.

Sunday.Monday.Tuesday.Wednesday.Thursday.Friday.Saturday

01|02|03|04|05|06|07|08|09|10|11|12|13|14|15|16|17|18|19|20|21|22|23|24|25|26|27|28|29|30

....
....
....
....
....
....
....
....
....
....
....
....
....
....
....
....
....
....
....
....
....
....
....
....
....
....
....
....
....
....
....
....
....

January. February. March. April. May. June. July. August. September. October. November. December.

Sunday. Monday. Tuesday. Wednesday. Thursday. Friday. Saturday

01|02|03|04|05|06|07|08|09|10|11|12|13|14|15|16|17|18|19|20|21|22|23|24|25|26|27|28|29|30

January. February. March. April. May. June. July. August. September. October. November. December.

Sunday. Monday. Tuesday. Wednesday. Thursday. Friday. Saturday

01|02|03|04|05|06|07|08|09|10|11|12|13|14|15|16|17|18|19|20|21|22|23|24|25|26|27|28|29|30

....
....
....
....
....
....
....
....
....
....
....
....
....
....
....
....
....
....
....
....
....
....
....
....
....
....
....
....
....
....
....

January. February. March. April. May. June. July. August. September. October. November. December.

Sunday. Monday. Tuesday. Wednesday. Thursday. Friday. Saturday

01|02|03|04|05|06|07|08|09|10|11|12|13|14|15|16|17|18|19|20|21|22|23|24|25|26|27|28|29|30

....

....

....

....

....

....

....

....

....

....

....

....

....

....

....

....

....

....

....

....

....

....

....

....

....

....

....

....

....

....

....

....

....

....

133

January.February.March.April.May.June.July.August.September.October.November.December.

Sunday.Monday.Tuesday.Wednesday.Thursday.Friday.Saturday

01|02|03|04|05|06|07|08|09|10|11|12|13|14|15|16|17|18|19|20|21|22|23|24|25|26|27|28|29|30

January. February. March. April. May. June. July. August. September. October. November. December.

Sunday. Monday. Tuesday. Wednesday. Thursday. Friday. Saturday

01|02|03|04|05|06|07|08|09|10|11|12|13|14|15|16|17|18|19|20|21|22|23|24|25|26|27|28|29|30

January. February. March. April. May. June. July. August. September. October. November. December.

Sunday. Monday. Tuesday. Wednesday. Thursday. Friday. Saturday

01|02|03|04|05|06|07|08|09|10|11|12|13|14|15|16|17|18|19|20|21|22|23|24|25|26|27|28|29|30

January. February. March. April. May. June. July. August. September. October. November. December.

Sunday. Monday. Tuesday. Wednesday. Thursday. Friday. Saturday

01|02|03|04|05|06|07|08|09|10|11|12|13|14|15|16|17|18|19|20|21|22|23|24|25|26|27|28|29|30

....

....

....

....

....

....

....

....

....

....

....

....

....

....

....

....

....

....

....

....

....

....

....

....

....

....

....

....

....

....

....

....

137

January. February. March. April. May. June. July. August. September. October. November. December.

Sunday. Monday. Tuesday. Wednesday. Thursday. Friday. Saturday

01|02|03|04|05|06|07|08|09|10|11|12|13|14|15|16|17|18|19|20|21|22|23|24|25|26|27|28|29|30

....

....

....

....

....

....

....

....

....

....

....

....

....

....

....

....

....

....

....

....

....

....

....

....

....

....

....

....

....

....

....

....

....

January. February. March. April. May. June. July. August. September. October. November. December.

Sunday. Monday. Tuesday. Wednesday. Thursday. Friday. Saturday

01|02|03|04|05|06|07|08|09|10|11|12|13|14|15|16|17|18|19|20|21|22|23|24|25|26|27|28|29|30

January. February. March. April. May. June. July. August. September. October. November. December.

Sunday. Monday. Tuesday. Wednesday. Thursday. Friday. Saturday

01|02|03|04|05|06|07|08|09|10|11|12|13|14|15|16|17|18|19|20|21|22|23|24|25|26|27|28|29|30

January. February. March. April. May. June July. August. September. October. November. December.

Sunday. Monday. Tuesday. Wednesday. Thursday. Friday. Saturday

01|02|03|04|05|06|07|08|09|10|11|12|13|14|15|16|17|18|19|20|21|22|23|24|25|26|27|28|29|30

January. February. March. April. May. June. July. August. September. October. November. December.

Sunday. Monday. Tuesday. Wednesday. Thursday. Friday. Saturday

01|02|03|04|05|06|07|08|09|10|11|12|13|14|15|16|17|18|19|20|21|22|23|24|25|26|27|28|29|30

....
....
....
....
....
....
....
....
....
....
....
....
....
....
....
....
....
....
....
....
....
....
....
....
....
....
....
....
....
....

January.February.March.April.May.June.July.August.September.October.November.December.

Sunday.Monday.Tuesday.Wednesday.Thursday.Friday.Saturday

01|02|03|04|05|06|07|08|09|10|11|12|13|14|15|16|17|18|19|20|21|22|23|24|25|26|27|28|29|30

January. February. March. April. May. June. July. August. September. October. November. December.

Sunday. Monday. Tuesday. Wednesday. Thursday. Friday. Saturday

01|02|03|04|05|06|07|08|09|10|11|12|13|14|15|16|17|18|19|20|21|22|23|24|25|26|27|28|29|30

....

....

....

....

....

....

....

....

....

....

....

....

....

....

....

....

....

....

....

....

....

....

....

....

....

....

....

....

....

January.February.March.April.May.June.July.August.September.October.November.December.

Sunday.Monday.Tuesday.Wednesday.Thursday.Friday.Saturday

01|02|03|04|05|06|07|08|09|10|11|12|13|14|15|16|17|18|19|20|21|22|23|24|25|26|27|28|29|30

January. February. March. April. May. June. July. August. September. October. November. December.

Sunday. Monday. Tuesday. Wednesday. Thursday. Friday. Saturday

01|02|03|04|05|06|07|08|09|10|11|12|13|14|15|16|17|18|19|20|21|22|23|24|25|26|27|28|29|30

....
....
....
....
....
....
....
....
....
....
....
....
....
....
....
....
....
....
....
....
....
....
....
....
....
....
....
....
....
....

January. February. March. April. May. June July. August. September. October. November. December.

Sunday. Monday. Tuesday. Wednesday. Thursday. Friday. Saturday

01|02|03|04|05|06|07|08|09|10|11|12|13|14|15|16|17|18|19|20|21|22|23|24|25|26|27|28|29|30

January. February. March. April. May. June. July. August. September. October. November. December.

Sunday. Monday. Tuesday. Wednesday. Thursday. Friday. Saturday

01|02|03|04|05|06|07|08|09|10|11|12|13|14|15|16|17|18|19|20|21|22|23|24|25|26|27|28|29|30

January. February. March. April. May. June. July. August. September. October. November. December.

Sunday. Monday. Tuesday. Wednesday. Thursday. Friday. Saturday

01|02|03|04|05|06|07|08|09|10|11|12|13|14|15|16|17|18|19|20|21|22|23|24|25|26|27|28|29|30

January. February. March. April. May. June. July. August. September. October. November. December.

Sunday. Monday. Tuesday. Wednesday. Thursday. Friday. Saturday

01|02|03|04|05|06|07|08|09|10|11|12|13|14|15|16|17|18|19|20|21|22|23|24|25|26|27|28|29|30

January. February. March. April. May. June. July. August. September. October. November. December.

Sunday. Monday. Tuesday. Wednesday. Thursday. Friday. Saturday

01|02|03|04|05|06|07|08|09|10|11|12|13|14|15|16|17|18|19|20|21|22|23|24|25|26|27|28|29|30

January. February. March. April. May. June. July. August. September. October. November. December.

Sunday. Monday. Tuesday. Wednesday. Thursday. Friday. Saturday

01|02|03|04|05|06|07|08|09|10|11|12|13|14|15|16|17|18|19|20|21|22|23|24|25|26|27|28|29|30

....

....

....

....

....

....

....

....

....

....

....

....

....

....

....

....

....

....

....

....

....

....

....

....

....

....

....

....

....

....

....

January. February. March. April. May. June. July. August. September. October. November. December.

Sunday. Monday. Tuesday. Wednesday. Thursday. Friday. Saturday

01|02|03|04|05|06|07|08|09|10|11|12|13|14|15|16|17|18|19|20|21|22|23|24|25|26|27|28|29|30

January. February. March. April. May. June. July. August. September. October. November. December.

Sunday. Monday. Tuesday. Wednesday. Thursday. Friday. Saturday

01|02|03|04|05|06|07|08|09|10|11|12|13|14|15|16|17|18|19|20|21|22|23|24|25|26|27|28|29|30

January. February. March. April. May. June. July. August. September. October. November. December.

Sunday. Monday. Tuesday. Wednesday. Thursday. Friday. Saturday

01|02|03|04|05|06|07|08|09|10|11|12|13|14|15|16|17|18|19|20|21|22|23|24|25|26|27|28|29|30

January. February. March. April. May. June. July. August. September. October. November. December.

Sunday. Monday. Tuesday. Wednesday. Thursday. Friday. Saturday

01|02|03|04|05|06|07|08|09|10|11|12|13|14|15|16|17|18|19|20|21|22|23|24|25|26|27|28|29|30

....

....

....

....

....

....

....

....

....

....

....

....

....

....

....

....

....

....

....

....

....

....

....

....

....

....

....

....

....

....

January. February. March. April. May. June. July. August. September. October. November. December.

Sunday. Monday. Tuesday. Wednesday. Thursday. Friday. Saturday

01|02|03|04|05|06|07|08|09|10|11|12|13|14|15|16|17|18|19|20|21|22|23|24|25|26|27|28|29|30

....

....

....

....

....

....

....

....

....

....

....

....

....

....

....

....

....

....

....

....

....

....

....

....

....

....

....

....

....

....

....

....

January. February. March. April. May. June. July. August. September. October. November. December.

Sunday. Monday. Tuesday. Wednesday. Thursday. Friday. Saturday

01|02|03|04|05|06|07|08|09|10|11|12|13|14|15|16|17|18|19|20|21|22|23|24|25|26|27|28|29|30

....

....

....

....

....

....

....

....

....

....

....

....

....

....

....

....

....

....

....

....

....

....

....

....

....

....

....

....

....

....

January. February. March. April. May. June. July. August. September. October. November. December.

Sunday. Monday. Tuesday. Wednesday. Thursday. Friday. Saturday

01|02|03|04|05|06|07|08|09|10|11|12|13|14|15|16|17|18|19|20|21|22|23|24|25|26|27|28|29|30

January. February. March. April. May. June. July. August. September. October. November. December.

Sunday. Monday. Tuesday. Wednesday. Thursday. Friday. Saturday

01|02|03|04|05|06|07|08|09|10|11|12|13|14|15|16|17|18|19|20|21|22|23|24|25|26|27|28|29|30

January. February. March. April. May. June. July. August. September. October. November. December.

Sunday. Monday. Tuesday. Wednesday. Thursday. Friday. Saturday

01|02|03|04|05|06|07|08|09|10|11|12|13|14|15|16|17|18|19|20|21|22|23|24|25|26|27|28|29|30

January. February. March. April. May. June. July. August. September. October. November. December.

Sunday. Monday. Tuesday. Wednesday. Thursday. Friday. Saturday

01|02|03|04|05|06|07|08|09|10|11|12|13|14|15|16|17|18|19|20|21|22|23|24|25|26|27|28|29|30

....

....

....

....

....

....

....

....

....

....

....

....

....

....

....

....

....

....

....

....

....

....

....

....

....

....

....

....

....

January. February. March. April. May. June. July. August. September. October. November. December.

Sunday. Monday. Tuesday. Wednesday. Thursday. Friday. Saturday

01|02|03|04|05|06|07|08|09|10|11|12|13|14|15|16|17|18|19|20|21|22|23|24|25|26|27|28|29|30

163

January. February. March. April. May. June. July. August. September. October. November. December.

Sunday. Monday. Tuesday. Wednesday. Thursday. Friday. Saturday

01|02|03|04|05|06|07|08|09|10|11|12|13|14|15|16|17|18|19|20|21|22|23|24|25|26|27|28|29|30

....
....
....
....
....
....
....
....
....
....
....
....
....
....
....
....
....
....
....
....
....
....
....
....
....
....
....
....
....
....
....

January.February.March.April.May.June.July.August.September.October.November.December.

Sunday.Monday.Tuesday.Wednesday.Thursday.Friday.Saturday

01|02|03|04|05|06|07|08|09|10|11|12|13|14|15|16|17|18|19|20|21|22|23|24|25|26|27|28|29|30

January. February. March. April. May. June. July. August. September. October. November. December.

Sunday. Monday. Tuesday. Wednesday. Thursday. Friday. Saturday

01|02|03|04|05|06|07|08|09|10|11|12|13|14|15|16|17|18|19|20|21|22|23|24|25|26|27|28|29|30

....
....
....
....
....
....
....
....
....
....
....
....
....
....
....
....
....
....
....
....
....
....
....
....
....
....
....
....
....
....
....
....

January. February. March. April. May. June. July. August. September. October. November. December.

Sunday. Monday. Tuesday. Wednesday. Thursday. Friday. Saturday

01|02|03|04|05|06|07|08|09|10|11|12|13|14|15|16|17|18|19|20|21|22|23|24|25|26|27|28|29|30

January. February. March. April. May. June. July. August. September. October. November. December.

Sunday. Monday. Tuesday. Wednesday. Thursday. Friday. Saturday

01|02|03|04|05|06|07|08|09|10|11|12|13|14|15|16|17|18|19|20|21|22|23|24|25|26|27|28|29|30

January.February.March.April.May.June.July.August.September.October.November.December.

Sunday.Monday.Tuesday.Wednesday.Thursday.Friday.Saturday

01|02|03|04|05|06|07|08|09|10|11|12|13|14|15|16|17|18|19|20|21|22|23|24|25|26|27|28|29|30

....

....

....

....

....

....

....

....

....

....

....

....

....

....

....

....

....

....

....

....

....

....

....

....

....

....

....

....

....

....

....

....

....

January. February. March. April. May. June. July. August. September. October. November. December.

Sunday. Monday. Tuesday. Wednesday. Thursday. Friday. Saturday

01|02|03|04|05|06|07|08|09|10|11|12|13|14|15|16|17|18|19|20|21|22|23|24|25|26|27|28|29|30

January. February. March. April. May. June. July. August. September. October. November. December.

Sunday. Monday. Tuesday. Wednesday. Thursday. Friday. Saturday

01|02|03|04|05|06|07|08|09|10|11|12|13|14|15|16|17|18|19|20|21|22|23|24|25|26|27|28|29|30

....

....

....

....

....

....

....

....

....

....

....

....

....

....

....

....

....

....

....

....

....

....

....

....

....

....

....

....

....

....

....

....

January.February.March.April.May.June.July.August.September.October.November.December.

Sunday.Monday.Tuesday.Wednesday.Thursday.Friday.Saturday

01|02|03|04|05|06|07|08|09|10|11|12|13|14|15|16|17|18|19|20|21|22|23|24|25|26|27|28|29|30

....

....

....

....

....

....

....

....

....

....

....

....

....

....

....

....

....

....

....

....

....

....

....

....

....

....

....

....

....

....

....

....

January. February. March. April. May. June. July. August. September. October. November. December.

Sunday. Monday. Tuesday. Wednesday. Thursday. Friday. Saturday

01|02|03|04|05|06|07|08|09|10|11|12|13|14|15|16|17|18|19|20|21|22|23|24|25|26|27|28|29|30

....
....
....
....
....
....
....
....
....
....
....
....
....
....
....
....
....
....
....
....
....
....
....
....
....
....
....
....
....
....
....
....
....
....
....

173

January. February. March. April. May. June. July. August. September. October. November. December.

Sunday. Monday. Tuesday. Wednesday. Thursday. Friday. Saturday

01|02|03|04|05|06|07|08|09|10|11|12|13|14|15|16|17|18|19|20|21|22|23|24|25|26|27|28|29|30

....
....
....
....
....
....
....
....
....
....
....
....
....
....
....
....
....
....
....
....
....
....
....
....
....
....
....
....
....
....

January. February. March. April. May. June. July. August. September. October. November. December.

Sunday. Monday. Tuesday. Wednesday. Thursday. Friday. Saturday

01|02|03|04|05|06|07|08|09|10|11|12|13|14|15|16|17|18|19|20|21|22|23|24|25|26|27|28|29|30

January. February. March. April. May. June. July. August. September. October. November. December.

Sunday. Monday. Tuesday. Wednesday. Thursday. Friday. Saturday

01|02|03|04|05|06|07|08|09|10|11|12|13|14|15|16|17|18|19|20|21|22|23|24|25|26|27|28|29|30

....

....

....

....

....

....

....

....

....

....

....

....

....

....

....

....

....

....

....

....

....

....

....

....

....

....

....

....

....

....

January. February. March. April. May. June. July. August. September. October. November. December.

Sunday. Monday. Tuesday. Wednesday. Thursday. Friday. Saturday

01|02|03|04|05|06|07|08|09|10|11|12|13|14|15|16|17|18|19|20|21|22|23|24|25|26|27|28|29|30

177

January. February. March. April. May. June. July. August. September. October. November. December.

Sunday. Monday. Tuesday. Wednesday. Thursday. Friday. Saturday

01|02|03|04|05|06|07|08|09|10|11|12|13|14|15|16|17|18|19|20|21|22|23|24|25|26|27|28|29|30

....

....

....

....

....

....

....

....

....

....

....

....

....

....

....

....

....

....

....

....

....

....

....

....

....

....

....

....

....

....

....

....

....

....

January. February. March. April. May. June. July. August. September. October. November. December.

Sunday. Monday. Tuesday. Wednesday. Thursday. Friday. Saturday

01|02|03|04|05|06|07|08|09|10|11|12|13|14|15|16|17|18|19|20|21|22|23|24|25|26|27|28|29|30

January. February. March. April. May. June. July. August. September. October. November. December.

Sunday. Monday. Tuesday. Wednesday. Thursday. Friday. Saturday

01|02|03|04|05|06|07|08|09|10|11|12|13|14|15|16|17|18|19|20|21|22|23|24|25|26|27|28|29|30

January. February. March. April. May. June. July. August. September. October. November. December.

Sunday. Monday. Tuesday. Wednesday. Thursday. Friday. Saturday

01|02|03|04|05|06|07|08|09|10|11|12|13|14|15|16|17|18|19|20|21|22|23|24|25|26|27|28|29|30

January. February. March. April. May. June. July. August. September. October. November. December.

Sunday. Monday. Tuesday. Wednesday. Thursday. Friday. Saturday

01|02|03|04|05|06|07|08|09|10|11|12|13|14|15|16|17|18|19|20|21|22|23|24|25|26|27|28|29|30

....
....
....
....
....
....
....
....
....
....
....
....
....
....
....
....
....
....
....
....
....
....
....
....
....
....
....
....
....
....
....

January. February. March. April. May. June. July. August. September. October. November. December.

Sunday. Monday. Tuesday. Wednesday. Thursday. Friday. Saturday

01|02|03|04|05|06|07|08|09|10|11|12|13|14|15|16|17|18|19|20|21|22|23|24|25|26|27|28|29|30

January.February.March.April.May.June.July.August.September.October.November.December.

Sunday.Monday.Tuesday.Wednesday.Thursday.Friday.Saturday

01|02|03|04|05|06|07|08|09|10|11|12|13|14|15|16|17|18|19|20|21|22|23|24|25|26|27|28|29|30

January.February.March.April.May.June.July.August.September.October.November.December.

Sunday.Monday.Tuesday.Wednesday.Thursday.Friday.Saturday

01|02|03|04|05|06|07|08|09|10|11|12|13|14|15|16|17|18|19|20|21|22|23|24|25|26|27|28|29|30

January.February.March.April.May.June.July.August.September.October.November.December.

Sunday.Monday.Tuesday.Wednesday.Thursday.Friday.Saturday

01|02|03|04|05|06|07|08|09|10|11|12|13|14|15|16|17|18|19|20|21|22|23|24|25|26|27|28|29|30

....
....
....
....
....
....
....
....
....
....
....
....
....
....
....
....
....
....
....
....
....
....
....
....
....
....
....
....
....
....
....

January. February. March. April. May. June. July. August. September. October. November. December.

Sunday. Monday. Tuesday. Wednesday. Thursday. Friday. Saturday

01|02|03|04|05|06|07|08|09|10|11|12|13|14|15|16|17|18|19|20|21|22|23|24|25|26|27|28|29|30

January. February. March. April. May. June. July. August. September. October. November. December.

Sunday. Monday. Tuesday. Wednesday. Thursday. Friday. Saturday

01|02|03|04|05|06|07|08|09|10|11|12|13|14|15|16|17|18|19|20|21|22|23|24|25|26|27|28|29|30

January. February. March. April. May. June. July. August. September. October. November. December.

Sunday. Monday. Tuesday. Wednesday. Thursday. Friday. Saturday

01|02|03|04|05|06|07|08|09|10|11|12|13|14|15|16|17|18|19|20|21|22|23|24|25|26|27|28|29|30

January. February. March. April. May. June. July. August. September. October. November. December.

Sunday. Monday. Tuesday. Wednesday. Thursday. Friday. Saturday

01|02|03|04|05|06|07|08|09|10|11|12|13|14|15|16|17|18|19|20|21|22|23|24|25|26|27|28|29|30

January. February. March. April. May. June. July. August. September. October. November. December.

Sunday. Monday. Tuesday. Wednesday. Thursday. Friday. Saturday

01|02|03|04|05|06|07|08|09|10|11|12|13|14|15|16|17|18|19|20|21|22|23|24|25|26|27|28|29|30

January. February. March. April. May. June. July. August. September. October. November. December.

Sunday. Monday. Tuesday. Wednesday. Thursday. Friday. Saturday

01|02|03|04|05|06|07|08|09|10|11|12|13|14|15|16|17|18|19|20|21|22|23|24|25|26|27|28|29|30

....

....

....

....

....

....

....

....

....

....

....

....

....

....

....

....

....

....

....

....

....

....

....

....

....

....

....

....

....

....

January. February. March. April. May. June. July. August. September. October. November. December.

Sunday. Monday. Tuesday. Wednesday. Thursday. Friday. Saturday

01|02|03|04|05|06|07|08|09|10|11|12|13|14|15|16|17|18|19|20|21|22|23|24|25|26|27|28|29|30

....
....
....
....
....
....
....
....
....
....
....
....
....
....
....
....
....
....
....
....
....
....
....
....
....
....
....
....
....
....
....
....

January. February. March. April. May. June. July. August. September. October. November. December.

Sunday. Monday. Tuesday. Wednesday. Thursday. Friday. Saturday

01|02|03|04|05|06|07|08|09|10|11|12|13|14|15|16|17|18|19|20|21|22|23|24|25|26|27|28|29|30

January. February. March. April. May. June. July. August. September. October. November. December.

Sunday. Monday. Tuesday. Wednesday. Thursday. Friday. Saturday

01|02|03|04|05|06|07|08|09|10|11|12|13|14|15|16|17|18|19|20|21|22|23|24|25|26|27|28|29|30

January.February.March.April.May.June.July.August.September.October.November.December.

Sunday.Monday.Tuesday.Wednesday.Thursday.Friday.Saturday

01|02|03|04|05|06|07|08|09|10|11|12|13|14|15|16|17|18|19|20|21|22|23|24|25|26|27|28|29|30

January. February. March. April. May. June. July. August. September. October. November. December.

Sunday. Monday. Tuesday. Wednesday. Thursday. Friday. Saturday

01|02|03|04|05|06|07|08|09|10|11|12|13|14|15|16|17|18|19|20|21|22|23|24|25|26|27|28|29|30

....

....

....

....

....

....

....

....

....

....

....

....

....

....

....

....

....

....

....

....

....

....

....

....

....

....

....

....

....

....

....

....

....

January. February. March. April. May. June. July. August. September. October. November. December.

Sunday. Monday. Tuesday. Wednesday. Thursday. Friday. Saturday

01|02|03|04|05|06|07|08|09|10|11|12|13|14|15|16|17|18|19|20|21|22|23|24|25|26|27|28|29|30

....

....

....

....

....

....

....

....

....

....

....

....

....

....

....

....

....

....

....

....

....

....

....

....

....

....

....

....

....

....

January. February. March. April. May. June. July. August. September. October. November. December.

Sunday. Monday. Tuesday. Wednesday. Thursday. Friday. Saturday

01|02|03|04|05|06|07|08|09|10|11|12|13|14|15|16|17|18|19|20|21|22|23|24|25|26|27|28|29|30

January. February. March. April. May. June. July. August. September. October. November. December.

Sunday. Monday. Tuesday. Wednesday. Thursday. Friday. Saturday

01|02|03|04|05|06|07|08|09|10|11|12|13|14|15|16|17|18|19|20|21|22|23|24|25|26|27|28|29|30

....

....

....

....

....

....

....

....

....

....

....

....

....

....

....

....

....

....

....

....

....

....

....

....

....

....

....

....

....

....

January. February. March. April. May. June. July. August. September. October. November. December.

Sunday. Monday. Tuesday. Wednesday. Thursday. Friday. Saturday

01|02|03|04|05|06|07|08|09|10|11|12|13|14|15|16|17|18|19|20|21|22|23|24|25|26|27|28|29|30

....
....
....
....
....
....
....
....
....
....
....
....
....
....
....
....
....
....
....
....
....
....
....
....
....
....
....
....
....
....

January. February. March. April. May. June. July. August. September. October. November. December.

Sunday. Monday. Tuesday. Wednesday. Thursday. Friday. Saturday

01|02|03|04|05|06|07|08|09|10|11|12|13|14|15|16|17|18|19|20|21|22|23|24|25|26|27|28|29|30

January. February. March. April. May. June. July. August. September. October. November. December.

Sunday. Monday. Tuesday. Wednesday. Thursday. Friday. Saturday

01|02|03|04|05|06|07|08|09|10|11|12|13|14|15|16|17|18|19|20|21|22|23|24|25|26|27|28|29|30

....

....

....

....

....

....

....

....

....

....

....

....

....

....

....

....

....

....

....

....

....

....

....

....

....

....

....

....

....

....

....

....

....

....

January. February. March. April. May. June. July. August. September. October. November. December.

Sunday. Monday. Tuesday. Wednesday. Thursday. Friday. Saturday

01|02|03|04|05|06|07|08|09|10|11|12|13|14|15|16|17|18|19|20|21|22|23|24|25|26|27|28|29|30

January. February. March. April. May. June. July. August. September. October. November. December.

Sunday. Monday. Tuesday. Wednesday. Thursday. Friday. Saturday

01|02|03|04|05|06|07|08|09|10|11|12|13|14|15|16|17|18|19|20|21|22|23|24|25|26|27|28|29|30

....

....

....

....

....

....

....

....

....

....

....

....

....

....

....

....

....

....

....

....

....

....

....

....

....

....

....

....

....

....

....

....

....

January. February. March. April. May. June. July. August. September. October. November. December.

Sunday. Monday. Tuesday. Wednesday. Thursday. Friday. Saturday

01|02|03|04|05|06|07|08|09|10|11|12|13|14|15|16|17|18|19|20|21|22|23|24|25|26|27|28|29|30

January.February.March.April.May.June.July.August.September.October.November.December.

Sunday.Monday.Tuesday.Wednesday.Thursday.Friday.Saturday

01|02|03|04|05|06|07|08|09|10|11|12|13|14|15|16|17|18|19|20|21|22|23|24|25|26|27|28|29|30

January. February. March. April. May. June. July. August. September. October. November. December.

Sunday. Monday. Tuesday. Wednesday. Thursday. Friday. Saturday

01|02|03|04|05|06|07|08|09|10|11|12|13|14|15|16|17|18|19|20|21|22|23|24|25|26|27|28|29|30

January.February.March.April.May.June.July.August.September.October.November.December.

Sunday.Monday.Tuesday.Wednesday.Thursday.Friday.Saturday

01|02|03|04|05|06|07|08|09|10|11|12|13|14|15|16|17|18|19|20|21|22|23|24|25|26|27|28|29|30

....
....
....
....
....
....
....
....
....
....
....
....
....
....
....
....
....
....
....
....
....
....
....
....
....
....
....
....
....
....
....

January. February. March. April. May. June. July. August. September. October. November. December.

Sunday. Monday. Tuesday. Wednesday. Thursday. Friday. Saturday

01|02|03|04|05|06|07|08|09|10|11|12|13|14|15|16|17|18|19|20|21|22|23|24|25|26|27|28|29|30

January. February. March. April. May. June. July. August. September. October. November. December.

Sunday. Monday. Tuesday. Wednesday. Thursday. Friday. Saturday

01|02|03|04|05|06|07|08|09|10|11|12|13|14|15|16|17|18|19|20|21|22|23|24|25|26|27|28|29|30

....

....

....

....

....

....

....

....

....

....

....

....

....

....

....

....

....

....

....

....

....

....

....

....

....

....

....

....

....

January. February. March. April. May. June. July. August. September. October. November. December.

Sunday. Monday. Tuesday. Wednesday. Thursday. Friday. Saturday

01|02|03|04|05|06|07|08|09|10|11|12|13|14|15|16|17|18|19|20|21|22|23|24|25|26|27|28|29|30

January. February. March. April. May. June. July. August. September. October. November. December.

Sunday. Monday. Tuesday. Wednesday. Thursday. Friday. Saturday

01|02|03|04|05|06|07|08|09|10|11|12|13|14|15|16|17|18|19|20|21|22|23|24|25|26|27|28|29|30

January. February. March. April. May. June. July. August. September. October. November. December.

Sunday. Monday. Tuesday. Wednesday. Thursday. Friday. Saturday

01|02|03|04|05|06|07|08|09|10|11|12|13|14|15|16|17|18|19|20|21|22|23|24|25|26|27|28|29|30

January. February. March. April. May. June. July. August. September. October. November. December.

Sunday. Monday. Tuesday. Wednesday. Thursday. Friday. Saturday

01|02|03|04|05|06|07|08|09|10|11|12|13|14|15|16|17|18|19|20|21|22|23|24|25|26|27|28|29|30

January. February. March. April. May. June. July. August. September. October. November. December.

Sunday. Monday. Tuesday. Wednesday. Thursday. Friday. Saturday

01|02|03|04|05|06|07|08|09|10|11|12|13|14|15|16|17|18|19|20|21|22|23|24|25|26|27|28|29|30

January. February. March. April. May. June. July. August. September. October. November. December.

Sunday. Monday. Tuesday. Wednesday. Thursday. Friday. Saturday

01|02|03|04|05|06|07|08|09|10|11|12|13|14|15|16|17|18|19|20|21|22|23|24|25|26|27|28|29|30

....
....
....
....
....
....
....
....
....
....
....
....
....
....
....
....
....
....
....
....
....
....
....
....
....
....
....
....
....
....
....
....

January. February. March. April. May. June. July. August. September. October. November. December.

Sunday. Monday. Tuesday. Wednesday. Thursday. Friday. Saturday

01|02|03|04|05|06|07|08|09|10|11|12|13|14|15|16|17|18|19|20|21|22|23|24|25|26|27|28|29|30

January. February. March. April. May. June. July. August. September. October. November. December.

Sunday. Monday. Tuesday. Wednesday. Thursday. Friday. Saturday

01|02|03|04|05|06|07|08|09|10|11|12|13|14|15|16|17|18|19|20|21|22|23|24|25|26|27|28|29|30

January. February. March. April. May. June. July. August. September. October. November. December.

Sunday. Monday. Tuesday. Wednesday. Thursday. Friday. Saturday

01|02|03|04|05|06|07|08|09|10|11|12|13|14|15|16|17|18|19|20|21|22|23|24|25|26|27|28|29|30

January. February. March. April. May. June. July. August. September. October. November. December.

Sunday. Monday. Tuesday. Wednesday. Thursday. Friday. Saturday

01|02|03|04|05|06|07|08|09|10|11|12|13|14|15|16|17|18|19|20|21|22|23|24|25|26|27|28|29|30

January. February. March. April. May. June. July. August. September. October. November. December.

Sunday. Monday. Tuesday. Wednesday. Thursday. Friday. Saturday

01|02|03|04|05|06|07|08|09|10|11|12|13|14|15|16|17|18|19|20|21|22|23|24|25|26|27|28|29|30

January. February. March. April. May. June. July. August. September. October. November. December.

Sunday. Monday. Tuesday. Wednesday. Thursday. Friday. Saturday

01|02|03|04|05|06|07|08|09|10|11|12|13|14|15|16|17|18|19|20|21|22|23|24|25|26|27|28|29|30

January. February. March. April. May. June. July. August. September. October. November. December.

Sunday. Monday. Tuesday. Wednesday. Thursday. Friday. Saturday

01|02|03|04|05|06|07|08|09|10|11|12|13|14|15|16|17|18|19|20|21|22|23|24|25|26|27|28|29|30

....
....
....
....
....
....
....
....
....
....
....
....
....
....
....
....
....
....
....
....
....
....
....
....
....
....
....
....
....
....

January. February. March. April. May. June. July. August. September. October. November. December.

Sunday. Monday. Tuesday. Wednesday. Thursday. Friday. Saturday

01|02|03|04|05|06|07|08|09|10|11|12|13|14|15|16|17|18|19|20|21|22|23|24|25|26|27|28|29|30

January. February. March. April. May. June. July. August. September. October. November. December.

Sunday. Monday. Tuesday. Wednesday. Thursday. Friday. Saturday

01|02|03|04|05|06|07|08|09|10|11|12|13|14|15|16|17|18|19|20|21|22|23|24|25|26|27|28|29|30

January. February. March. April. May. June. July. August. September. October. November. December.

Sunday. Monday. Tuesday. Wednesday. Thursday. Friday. Saturday

01|02|03|04|05|06|07|08|09|10|11|12|13|14|15|16|17|18|19|20|21|22|23|24|25|26|27|28|29|30

January. February. March. April. May. June. July. August. September. October. November. December.

Sunday. Monday. Tuesday. Wednesday. Thursday. Friday. Saturday

01|02|03|04|05|06|07|08|09|10|11|12|13|14|15|16|17|18|19|20|21|22|23|24|25|26|27|28|29|30

January. February. March. April. May. June. July. August. September. October. November. December.

Sunday. Monday. Tuesday. Wednesday. Thursday. Friday. Saturday

01|02|03|04|05|06|07|08|09|10|11|12|13|14|15|16|17|18|19|20|21|22|23|24|25|26|27|28|29|30

January. February. March. April. May. June. July. August. September. October. November. December.

Sunday. Monday. Tuesday. Wednesday. Thursday. Friday. Saturday

01|02|03|04|05|06|07|08|09|10|11|12|13|14|15|16|17|18|19|20|21|22|23|24|25|26|27|28|29|30

....

....

....

....

....

....

....

....

....

....

....

....

....

....

....

....

....

....

....

....

....

....

....

....

....

....

....

....

....

....

....

January. February. March. April. May. June. July. August. September. October. November. December.

Sunday. Monday. Tuesday. Wednesday. Thursday. Friday. Saturday

01|02|03|04|05|06|07|08|09|10|11|12|13|14|15|16|17|18|19|20|21|22|23|24|25|26|27|28|29|30

January. February. March. April. May. June. July. August. September. October. November. December.

Sunday. Monday. Tuesday. Wednesday. Thursday. Friday. Saturday

01|02|03|04|05|06|07|08|09|10|11|12|13|14|15|16|17|18|19|20|21|22|23|24|25|26|27|28|29|30

January. February. March. April. May. June. July. August. September. October. November. December.

Sunday. Monday. Tuesday. Wednesday. Thursday. Friday. Saturday

01|02|03|04|05|06|07|08|09|10|11|12|13|14|15|16|17|18|19|20|21|22|23|24|25|26|27|28|29|30

January. February. March. April. May. June. July. August. September. October. November. December.

Sunday. Monday. Tuesday. Wednesday. Thursday. Friday. Saturday

01|02|03|04|05|06|07|08|09|10|11|12|13|14|15|16|17|18|19|20|21|22|23|24|25|26|27|28|29|30

January. February. March. April. May. June. July. August. September. October. November. December.

Sunday. Monday. Tuesday. Wednesday. Thursday. Friday. Saturday

01|02|03|04|05|06|07|08|09|10|11|12|13|14|15|16|17|18|19|20|21|22|23|24|25|26|27|28|29|30

....

....

....

....

....

....

....

....

....

....

....

....

....

....

....

....

....

....

....

....

....

....

....

....

....

....

....

....

....

....

....

....

....

January. February. March. April. May. June. July. August. September. October. November. December.

Sunday. Monday. Tuesday. Wednesday. Thursday. Friday. Saturday

01|02|03|04|05|06|07|08|09|10|11|12|13|14|15|16|17|18|19|20|21|22|23|24|25|26|27|28|29|30

January. February. March. April. May. June. July. August. September. October. November. December.

Sunday. Monday. Tuesday. Wednesday. Thursday. Friday. Saturday

01|02|03|04|05|06|07|08|09|10|11|12|13|14|15|16|17|18|19|20|21|22|23|24|25|26|27|28|29|30

237

January. February. March. April. May. June. July. August. September. October. November. December.

Sunday. Monday. Tuesday. Wednesday. Thursday. Friday. Saturday

01|02|03|04|05|06|07|08|09|10|11|12|13|14|15|16|17|18|19|20|21|22|23|24|25|26|27|28|29|30

January.February.March.April.May.June.July.August.September.October.November.December.

Sunday.Monday.Tuesday.Wednesday.Thursday.Friday.Saturday

01|02|03|04|05|06|07|08|09|10|11|12|13|14|15|16|17|18|19|20|21|22|23|24|25|26|27|28|29|30

January. February. March. April. May. June. July. August. September. October. November. December.

Sunday. Monday. Tuesday. Wednesday. Thursday. Friday. Saturday

01|02|03|04|05|06|07|08|09|10|11|12|13|14|15|16|17|18|19|20|21|22|23|24|25|26|27|28|29|30

January. February. March. April. May. June. July. August. September. October. November. December.

Sunday. Monday. Tuesday. Wednesday. Thursday. Friday. Saturday

01|02|03|04|05|06|07|08|09|10|11|12|13|14|15|16|17|18|19|20|21|22|23|24|25|26|27|28|29|30

241

January. February. March. April. May. June. July. August. September. October. November. December.

Sunday. Monday. Tuesday. Wednesday. Thursday. Friday. Saturday

01|02|03|04|05|06|07|08|09|10|11|12|13|14|15|16|17|18|19|20|21|22|23|24|25|26|27|28|29|30

....

....

....

....

....

....

....

....

....

....

....

....

....

....

....

....

....

....

....

....

....

....

....

....

....

....

....

....

....

....

January. February. March. April. May. June. July. August. September. October. November. December.

Sunday. Monday. Tuesday. Wednesday. Thursday. Friday. Saturday

01|02|03|04|05|06|07|08|09|10|11|12|13|14|15|16|17|18|19|20|21|22|23|24|25|26|27|28|29|30

January. February. March. April. May. June. July. August. September. October. November. December.

Sunday. Monday. Tuesday. Wednesday. Thursday. Friday. Saturday

01|02|03|04|05|06|07|08|09|10|11|12|13|14|15|16|17|18|19|20|21|22|23|24|25|26|27|28|29|30

....

....

....

....

....

....

....

....

....

....

....

....

....

....

....

....

....

....

....

....

....

....

....

....

....

....

....

....

....

....

January. February. March. April. May. June. July. August. September. October. November. December.

Sunday. Monday. Tuesday. Wednesday. Thursday. Friday. Saturday

01|02|03|04|05|06|07|08|09|10|11|12|13|14|15|16|17|18|19|20|21|22|23|24|25|26|27|28|29|30

....
....
....
....
....
....
....
....
....
....
....
....
....
....
....
....
....
....
....
....
....
....
....
....
....
....
....
....
....
....
....
....

January. February. March. April. May. June. July. August. September. October. November. December.

Sunday. Monday. Tuesday. Wednesday. Thursday. Friday. Saturday

01|02|03|04|05|06|07|08|09|10|11|12|13|14|15|16|17|18|19|20|21|22|23|24|25|26|27|28|29|30

January.February.March.April.May.June.July.August.September.October.November.December.

Sunday.Monday.Tuesday.Wednesday.Thursday.Friday.Saturday

01|02|03|04|05|06|07|08|09|10|11|12|13|14|15|16|17|18|19|20|21|22|23|24|25|26|27|28|29|30

....

....

....

....

....

....

....

....

....

....

....

....

....

....

....

....

....

....

....

....

....

....

....

....

....

....

....

....

....

....

....

....

....

....

January. February. March. April. May. June. July. August. September. October. November. December.

Sunday. Monday. Tuesday. Wednesday. Thursday. Friday. Saturday

01|02|03|04|05|06|07|08|09|10|11|12|13|14|15|16|17|18|19|20|21|22|23|24|25|26|27|28|29|30

....
....
....
....
....
....
....
....
....
....
....
....
....
....
....
....
....
....
....
....
....
....
....
....
....
....
....
....
....
....

January. February. March. April. May. June. July. August. September. October. November. December.

Sunday. Monday. Tuesday. Wednesday. Thursday. Friday. Saturday

01|02|03|04|05|06|07|08|09|10|11|12|13|14|15|16|17|18|19|20|21|22|23|24|25|26|27|28|29|30

January. February. March. April. May. June. July. August. September. October. November. December.

Sunday. Monday. Tuesday. Wednesday. Thursday. Friday. Saturday

01|02|03|04|05|06|07|08|09|10|11|12|13|14|15|16|17|18|19|20|21|22|23|24|25|26|27|28|29|30

....

....

....

....

....

....

....

....

....

....

....

....

....

....

....

....

....

....

....

....

....

....

....

....

....

....

....

....

....

....

January. February. March. April. May. June. July. August. September. October. November. December.

Sunday. Monday. Tuesday. Wednesday. Thursday. Friday. Saturday

01|02|03|04|05|06|07|08|09|10|11|12|13|14|15|16|17|18|19|20|21|22|23|24|25|26|27|28|29|30

January. February. March. April. May. June. July. August. September. October. November. December.

Sunday. Monday. Tuesday. Wednesday. Thursday. Friday. Saturday

01|02|03|04|05|06|07|08|09|10|11|12|13|14|15|16|17|18|19|20|21|22|23|24|25|26|27|28|29|30

....
....
....
....
....
....
....
....
....
....
....
....
....
....
....
....
....
....
....
....
....
....
....
....
....
....
....
....
....
....

January.February.March.April.May.June.July.August.September.October.November.December.

Sunday.Monday.Tuesday.Wednesday.Thursday.Friday.Saturday

01|02|03|04|05|06|07|08|09|10|11|12|13|14|15|16|17|18|19|20|21|22|23|24|25|26|27|28|29|30

January, February, March, April, May, June, July, August, September, October, November, December.

Sunday, Monday, Tuesday, Wednesday, Thursday, Friday, Saturday

01|02|03|04|05|06|07|08|09|10|11|12|13|14|15|16|17|18|19|20|21|22|23|24|25|26|27|28|29|30

January. February. March. April. May. June. July. August. September. October. November. December.

Sunday. Monday. Tuesday. Wednesday. Thursday. Friday. Saturday

01|02|03|04|05|06|07|08|09|10|11|12|13|14|15|16|17|18|19|20|21|22|23|24|25|26|27|28|29|30

255

January. February. March. April. May. June. July. August. September. October. November. December.

Sunday. Monday. Tuesday. Wednesday. Thursday. Friday. Saturday

01|02|03|04|05|06|07|08|09|10|11|12|13|14|15|16|17|18|19|20|21|22|23|24|25|26|27|28|29|30

January. February. March. April. May. June. July. August. September. October. November. December.

Sunday. Monday. Tuesday. Wednesday. Thursday. Friday. Saturday

01|02|03|04|05|06|07|08|09|10|11|12|13|14|15|16|17|18|19|20|21|22|23|24|25|26|27|28|29|30

....

....

....

....

....

....

....

....

....

....

....

....

....

....

....

....

....

....

....

....

....

....

....

....

....

....

....

....

....

....

....

....

....

....

257

January. February. March. April. May. June. July. August. September. October. November. December.

Sunday. Monday. Tuesday. Wednesday. Thursday. Friday. Saturday

01|02|03|04|05|06|07|08|09|10|11|12|13|14|15|16|17|18|19|20|21|22|23|24|25|26|27|28|29|30

....

....

....

....

....

....

....

....

....

....

....

....

....

....

....

....

....

....

....

....

....

....

....

....

....

....

....

....

....

....

January. February. March. April. May. June. July. August. September. October. November. December.

Sunday. Monday. Tuesday. Wednesday. Thursday. Friday. Saturday

01|02|03|04|05|06|07|08|09|10|11|12|13|14|15|16|17|18|19|20|21|22|23|24|25|26|27|28|29|30

January. February. March. April. May. June. July. August. September. October. November. December.

Sunday. Monday. Tuesday. Wednesday. Thursday. Friday. Saturday

01|02|03|04|05|06|07|08|09|10|11|12|13|14|15|16|17|18|19|20|21|22|23|24|25|26|27|28|29|30

January. February. March. April. May. June. July. August. September. October. November. December.

Sunday. Monday. Tuesday. Wednesday. Thursday. Friday. Saturday

01|02|03|04|05|06|07|08|09|10|11|12|13|14|15|16|17|18|19|20|21|22|23|24|25|26|27|28|29|30

January. February. March. April. May. June. July. August. September. October. November. December.

Sunday. Monday. Tuesday. Wednesday. Thursday. Friday. Saturday

01|02|03|04|05|06|07|08|09|10|11|12|13|14|15|16|17|18|19|20|21|22|23|24|25|26|27|28|29|30

January. February. March. April. May. June. July. August. September. October. November. December.

Sunday. Monday. Tuesday. Wednesday. Thursday. Friday. Saturday

01|02|03|04|05|06|07|08|09|10|11|12|13|14|15|16|17|18|19|20|21|22|23|24|25|26|27|28|29|30

January.February.March.April.May.June.July.August.September.October.November.December.

Sunday.Monday.Tuesday.Wednesday.Thursday.Friday.Saturday

01|02|03|04|05|06|07|08|09|10|11|12|13|14|15|16|17|18|19|20|21|22|23|24|25|26|27|28|29|30

January. February. March. April. May. June. July. August. September. October. November. December.

Sunday. Monday. Tuesday. Wednesday. Thursday. Friday. Saturday

01|02|03|04|05|06|07|08|09|10|11|12|13|14|15|16|17|18|19|20|21|22|23|24|25|26|27|28|29|30

January, February, March, April, May, June, July, August, September, October, November, December.

Sunday, Monday, Tuesday, Wednesday, Thursday, Friday, Saturday

01|02|03|04|05|06|07|08|09|10|11|12|13|14|15|16|17|18|19|20|21|22|23|24|25|26|27|28|29|30

January. February. March. April. May. June. July. August. September. October. November. December.

Sunday. Monday. Tuesday. Wednesday. Thursday. Friday. Saturday

01|02|03|04|05|06|07|08|09|10|11|12|13|14|15|16|17|18|19|20|21|22|23|24|25|26|27|28|29|30

January. February. March. April. May. June. July. August. September. October. November. December.

Sunday. Monday. Tuesday. Wednesday. Thursday. Friday. Saturday

01|02|03|04|05|06|07|08|09|10|11|12|13|14|15|16|17|18|19|20|21|22|23|24|25|26|27|28|29|30

....
....
....
....
....
....
....
....
....
....
....
....
....
....
....
....
....
....
....
....
....
....
....
....
....
....
....
....
....
....
....

January. February. March. April. May. June. July. August. September. October. November. December.

Sunday. Monday. Tuesday. Wednesday. Thursday. Friday. Saturday

01|02|03|04|05|06|07|08|09|10|11|12|13|14|15|16|17|18|19|20|21|22|23|24|25|26|27|28|29|30

January. February. March. April. May. June. July. August. September. October. November. December.

Sunday. Monday. Tuesday. Wednesday. Thursday. Friday. Saturday

01|02|03|04|05|06|07|08|09|10|11|12|13|14|15|16|17|18|19|20|21|22|23|24|25|26|27|28|29|30

January. February. March. April. May. June. July. August. September. October. November. December.

Sunday. Monday. Tuesday. Wednesday. Thursday. Friday. Saturday

01|02|03|04|05|06|07|08|09|10|11|12|13|14|15|16|17|18|19|20|21|22|23|24|25|26|27|28|29|30

January. February. March. April. May. June. July. August. September. October. November. December.

Sunday. Monday. Tuesday. Wednesday. Thursday. Friday. Saturday

01|02|03|04|05|06|07|08|09|10|11|12|13|14|15|16|17|18|19|20|21|22|23|24|25|26|27|28|29|30

January.February.March.April.May.June.July.August.September.October.November.December.

Sunday.Monday.Tuesday.Wednesday.Thursday.Friday.Saturday

01|02|03|04|05|06|07|08|09|10|11|12|13|14|15|16|17|18|19|20|21|22|23|24|25|26|27|28|29|30

January. February. March. April. May. June. July. August. September. October. November. December.

Sunday. Monday. Tuesday. Wednesday. Thursday. Friday. Saturday

01|02|03|04|05|06|07|08|09|10|11|12|13|14|15|16|17|18|19|20|21|22|23|24|25|26|27|28|29|30

January. February. March. April. May. June. July. August. September. October. November. December.

Sunday. Monday. Tuesday. Wednesday. Thursday. Friday. Saturday

01|02|03|04|05|06|07|08|09|10|11|12|13|14|15|16|17|18|19|20|21|22|23|24|25|26|27|28|29|30

January.February.March.April.May.June.July.August.September.October.November.December.

Sunday.Monday.Tuesday.Wednesday.Thursday.Friday.Saturday

01|02|03|04|05|06|07|08|09|10|11|12|13|14|15|16|17|18|19|20|21|22|23|24|25|26|27|28|29|30

....

....

....

....

....

....

....

....

....

....

....

....

....

....

....

....

....

....

....

....

....

....

....

....

....

....

....

....

....

....

January. February. March. April. May. June. July. August. September. October. November. December.

Sunday. Monday. Tuesday. Wednesday. Thursday. Friday. Saturday

01|02|03|04|05|06|07|08|09|10|11|12|13|14|15|16|17|18|19|20|21|22|23|24|25|26|27|28|29|30

January. February. March. April. May. June. July. August. September. October. November. December.

Sunday. Monday. Tuesday. Wednesday. Thursday. Friday. Saturday

01|02|03|04|05|06|07|08|09|10|11|12|13|14|15|16|17|18|19|20|21|22|23|24|25|26|27|28|29|30

....
....
....
....
....
....
....
....
....
....
....
....
....
....
....
....
....
....
....
....
....
....
....
....
....
....
....
....
....
....
....

January. February. March. April. May. June. July. August. September. October. November. December.

Sunday. Monday. Tuesday. Wednesday. Thursday. Friday. Saturday

01|02|03|04|05|06|07|08|09|10|11|12|13|14|15|16|17|18|19|20|21|22|23|24|25|26|27|28|29|30

279

January. February. March. April. May. June. July. August. September. October. November. December.

Sunday. Monday. Tuesday. Wednesday. Thursday. Friday. Saturday

01|02|03|04|05|06|07|08|09|10|11|12|13|14|15|16|17|18|19|20|21|22|23|24|25|26|27|28|29|30

January. February. March. April. May. June. July. August. September. October. November. December.

Sunday. Monday. Tuesday. Wednesday. Thursday. Friday. Saturday

01|02|03|04|05|06|07|08|09|10|11|12|13|14|15|16|17|18|19|20|21|22|23|24|25|26|27|28|29|30

January. February. March. April. May. June. July. August. September. October. November. December.

Sunday. Monday. Tuesday. Wednesday. Thursday. Friday. Saturday

01|02|03|04|05|06|07|08|09|10|11|12|13|14|15|16|17|18|19|20|21|22|23|24|25|26|27|28|29|30

....
....
....
....
....
....
....
....
....
....
....
....
....
....
....
....
....
....
....
....
....
....
....
....
....
....
....
....
....
....
....
....
....

January. February. March. April. May. June. July. August. September. October. November. December.

Sunday. Monday. Tuesday. Wednesday. Thursday. Friday. Saturday

01|02|03|04|05|06|07|08|09|10|11|12|13|14|15|16|17|18|19|20|21|22|23|24|25|26|27|28|29|30

January. February. March. April. May. June. July. August. September. October. November. December.

Sunday. Monday. Tuesday. Wednesday. Thursday. Friday. Saturday

01|02|03|04|05|06|07|08|09|10|11|12|13|14|15|16|17|18|19|20|21|22|23|24|25|26|27|28|29|30

....
....
....
....
....
....
....
....
....
....
....
....
....
....
....
....
....
....
....
....
....
....
....
....
....
....
....
....
....
....
....
....

January. February. March. April. May. June. July. August. September. October. November. December.

Sunday. Monday. Tuesday. Wednesday. Thursday. Friday. Saturday

01|02|03|04|05|06|07|08|09|10|11|12|13|14|15|16|17|18|19|20|21|22|23|24|25|26|27|28|29|30

January.February.March.April.May.June.July.August.September.October.November.December.

Sunday.Monday.Tuesday.Wednesday.Thursday.Friday.Saturday

01|02|03|04|05|06|07|08|09|10|11|12|13|14|15|16|17|18|19|20|21|22|23|24|25|26|27|28|29|30

January. February. March. April. May. June. July. August. September. October. November. December.

Sunday. Monday. Tuesday. Wednesday. Thursday. Friday. Saturday

01|02|03|04|05|06|07|08|09|10|11|12|13|14|15|16|17|18|19|20|21|22|23|24|25|26|27|28|29|30

January. February. March. April. May. June. July. August. September. October. November. December.

Sunday. Monday. Tuesday. Wednesday. Thursday. Friday. Saturday

01|02|03|04|05|06|07|08|09|10|11|12|13|14|15|16|17|18|19|20|21|22|23|24|25|26|27|28|29|30

January.February.March.April.May.June.July.August.September.October.November.December.

Sunday.Monday.Tuesday.Wednesday.Thursday.Friday.Saturday

01|02|03|04|05|06|07|08|09|10|11|12|13|14|15|16|17|18|19|20|21|22|23|24|25|26|27|28|29|30

January. February. March. April. May. June. July. August. September. October. November. December.

Sunday. Monday. Tuesday. Wednesday. Thursday. Friday. Saturday

01|02|03|04|05|06|07|08|09|10|11|12|13|14|15|16|17|18|19|20|21|22|23|24|25|26|27|28|29|30

January. February. March. April. May. June. July. August. September. October. November. December.

Sunday. Monday. Tuesday. Wednesday. Thursday. Friday. Saturday

01|02|03|04|05|06|07|08|09|10|11|12|13|14|15|16|17|18|19|20|21|22|23|24|25|26|27|28|29|30

January. February. March. April. May. June. July. August. September. October. November. December.

Sunday. Monday. Tuesday. Wednesday. Thursday. Friday. Saturday

01|02|03|04|05|06|07|08|09|10|11|12|13|14|15|16|17|18|19|20|21|22|23|24|25|26|27|28|29|30

January. February. March. April. May. June. July. August. September. October. November. December.

Sunday. Monday. Tuesday. Wednesday. Thursday. Friday. Saturday

01|02|03|04|05|06|07|08|09|10|11|12|13|14|15|16|17|18|19|20|21|22|23|24|25|26|27|28|29|30

January. February. March. April. May. June. July. August. September. October. November. December.

Sunday. Monday. Tuesday. Wednesday. Thursday. Friday. Saturday

01|02|03|04|05|06|07|08|09|10|11|12|13|14|15|16|17|18|19|20|21|22|23|24|25|26|27|28|29|30

January. February. March. April. May. June. July. August. September. October. November. December.

Sunday. Monday. Tuesday. Wednesday. Thursday. Friday. Saturday

01|02|03|04|05|06|07|08|09|10|11|12|13|14|15|16|17|18|19|20|21|22|23|24|25|26|27|28|29|30

January. February. March. April. May. June. July. August. September. October. November. December.

Sunday. Monday. Tuesday. Wednesday. Thursday. Friday. Saturday

01|02|03|04|05|06|07|08|09|10|11|12|13|14|15|16|17|18|19|20|21|22|23|24|25|26|27|28|29|30

January. February. March. April. May. June. July. August. September. October. November. December.

Sunday. Monday. Tuesday. Wednesday. Thursday. Friday. Saturday

01|02|03|04|05|06|07|08|09|10|11|12|13|14|15|16|17|18|19|20|21|22|23|24|25|26|27|28|29|30

January. February. March. April. May. June. July. August. September. October. November. December.

Sunday. Monday. Tuesday. Wednesday. Thursday. Friday. Saturday

01|02|03|04|05|06|07|08|09|10|11|12|13|14|15|16|17|18|19|20|21|22|23|24|25|26|27|28|29|30

January. February. March. April. May. June. July. August. September. October. November. December.

Sunday. Monday. Tuesday. Wednesday. Thursday. Friday. Saturday

01|02|03|04|05|06|07|08|09|10|11|12|13|14|15|16|17|18|19|20|21|22|23|24|25|26|27|28|29|30

January. February. March. April. May. June. July. August. September. October. November. December.

Sunday. Monday. Tuesday. Wednesday. Thursday. Friday. Saturday

01|02|03|04|05|06|07|08|09|10|11|12|13|14|15|16|17|18|19|20|21|22|23|24|25|26|27|28|29|30

January. February. March. April. May. June. July. August. September. October. November. December.

Sunday. Monday. Tuesday. Wednesday. Thursday. Friday. Saturday

01|02|03|04|05|06|07|08|09|10|11|12|13|14|15|16|17|18|19|20|21|22|23|24|25|26|27|28|29|30

January.February.March.April.May.June.July.August.September.October.November.December.

Sunday.Monday.Tuesday.Wednesday.Thursday.Friday.Saturday

01|02|03|04|05|06|07|08|09|10|11|12|13|14|15|16|17|18|19|20|21|22|23|24|25|26|27|28|29|30

January. February. March. April. May. June. July. August. September. October. November. December.

Sunday. Monday. Tuesday. Wednesday. Thursday. Friday. Saturday

01|02|03|04|05|06|07|08|09|10|11|12|13|14|15|16|17|18|19|20|21|22|23|24|25|26|27|28|29|30

January. February. March. April. May. June. July. August. September. October. November. December.

Sunday. Monday. Tuesday. Wednesday. Thursday. Friday. Saturday

01|02|03|04|05|06|07|08|09|10|11|12|13|14|15|16|17|18|19|20|21|22|23|24|25|26|27|28|29|30

January. February. March. April. May. June. July. August. September. October. November. December.

Sunday. Monday. Tuesday. Wednesday. Thursday. Friday. Saturday

01|02|03|04|05|06|07|08|09|10|11|12|13|14|15|16|17|18|19|20|21|22|23|24|25|26|27|28|29|30

January. February. March. April. May. June. July. August. September. October. November. December.

Sunday. Monday. Tuesday. Wednesday. Thursday. Friday. Saturday

01|02|03|04|05|06|07|08|09|10|11|12|13|14|15|16|17|18|19|20|21|22|23|24|25|26|27|28|29|30

....
....
....
....
....
....
....
....
....
....
....
....
....
....
....
....
....
....
....
....
....
....
....
....
....
....
....
....
....

January. February. March. April. May. June. July. August. September. October. November. December.

Sunday. Monday. Tuesday. Wednesday. Thursday. Friday. Saturday

01|02|03|04|05|06|07|08|09|10|11|12|13|14|15|16|17|18|19|20|21|22|23|24|25|26|27|28|29|30

January.February.March.April.May.June.July.August.September.October.November.December.

Sunday.Monday.Tuesday.Wednesday.Thursday.Friday.Saturday

01|02|03|04|05|06|07|08|09|10|11|12|13|14|15|16|17|18|19|20|21|22|23|24|25|26|27|28|29|30

January. February. March. April. May. June. July. August. September. October. November. December.

Sunday. Monday. Tuesday. Wednesday. Thursday. Friday. Saturday

01|02|03|04|05|06|07|08|09|10|11|12|13|14|15|16|17|18|19|20|21|22|23|24|25|26|27|28|29|30

January. February. March. April. May. June. July. August. September. October. November. December.

Sunday. Monday. Tuesday. Wednesday. Thursday. Friday. Saturday

01|02|03|04|05|06|07|08|09|10|11|12|13|14|15|16|17|18|19|20|21|22|23|24|25|26|27|28|29|30

January. February. March. April. May. June. July. August. September. October. November. December.

Sunday. Monday. Tuesday. Wednesday. Thursday. Friday. Saturday

01|02|03|04|05|06|07|08|09|10|11|12|13|14|15|16|17|18|19|20|21|22|23|24|25|26|27|28|29|30

....

....

....

....

....

....

....

....

....

....

....

....

....

....

....

....

....

....

....

....

....

....

....

....

....

....

....

....

....

....

....

....

....

....

January. February. March. April. May. June. July. August. September. October. November. December.

Sunday. Monday. Tuesday. Wednesday. Thursday. Friday. Saturday

01|02|03|04|05|06|07|08|09|10|11|12|13|14|15|16|17|18|19|20|21|22|23|24|25|26|27|28|29|30

....
....
....
....
....
....
....
....
....
....
....
....
....
....
....
....
....
....
....
....
....
....
....
....
....
....
....
....
....
....
....
....
....

January. February. March. April. May. June. July. August. September. October. November. December.

Sunday. Monday. Tuesday. Wednesday. Thursday. Friday. Saturday

01|02|03|04|05|06|07|08|09|10|11|12|13|14|15|16|17|18|19|20|21|22|23|24|25|26|27|28|29|30

....

....

....

....

....

....

....

....

....

....

....

....

....

....

....

....

....

....

....

....

....

....

....

....

....

....

....

....

....

....

....

....

....

....

January. February. March. April. May. June. July. August. September. October. November. December.

Sunday. Monday. Tuesday. Wednesday. Thursday. Friday. Saturday

01|02|03|04|05|06|07|08|09|10|11|12|13|14|15|16|17|18|19|20|21|22|23|24|25|26|27|28|29|30

....

....

....

....

....

....

....

....

....

....

....

....

....

....

....

....

....

....

....

....

....

....

....

....

....

....

....

....

....

....

January. February. March. April. May. June. July. August. September. October. November. December.

Sunday. Monday. Tuesday. Wednesday. Thursday. Friday. Saturday

01|02|03|04|05|06|07|08|09|10|11|12|13|14|15|16|17|18|19|20|21|22|23|24|25|26|27|28|29|30

January. February. March. April. May. June. July. August. September. October. November. December.

Sunday. Monday. Tuesday. Wednesday. Thursday. Friday. Saturday

01|02|03|04|05|06|07|08|09|10|11|12|13|14|15|16|17|18|19|20|21|22|23|24|25|26|27|28|29|30

January. February. March. April. May. June. July. August. September. October. November. December.

Sunday. Monday. Tuesday. Wednesday. Thursday. Friday. Saturday

01|02|03|04|05|06|07|08|09|10|11|12|13|14|15|16|17|18|19|20|21|22|23|24|25|26|27|28|29|30

January. February. March. April. May. June. July. August. September. October. November. December.

Sunday. Monday. Tuesday. Wednesday. Thursday. Friday. Saturday

01|02|03|04|05|06|07|08|09|10|11|12|13|14|15|16|17|18|19|20|21|22|23|24|25|26|27|28|29|30

....
....
....
....
....
....
....
....
....
....
....
....
....
....
....
....
....
....
....
....
....
....
....
....
....
....
....
....
....
....

January. February. March. April. May. June. July. August. September. October. November. December.

Sunday. Monday. Tuesday. Wednesday. Thursday. Friday. Saturday

01|02|03|04|05|06|07|08|09|10|11|12|13|14|15|16|17|18|19|20|21|22|23|24|25|26|27|28|29|30

....
....
....
....
....
....
....
....
....
....
....
....
....
....
....
....
....
....
....
....
....
....
....
....
....
....
....
....
....
....
....
....

January. February. March. April. May. June. July. August. September. October. November. December.

Sunday. Monday. Tuesday. Wednesday. Thursday. Friday. Saturday

01|02|03|04|05|06|07|08|09|10|11|12|13|14|15|16|17|18|19|20|21|22|23|24|25|26|27|28|29|30

....

....

....

....

....

....

....

....

....

....

....

....

....

....

....

....

....

....

....

....

....

....

....

....

....

....

....

....

....

....

January. February. March. April. May. June. July. August. September. October. November. December.

Sunday. Monday. Tuesday. Wednesday. Thursday. Friday. Saturday

01|02|03|04|05|06|07|08|09|10|11|12|13|14|15|16|17|18|19|20|21|22|23|24|25|26|27|28|29|30

January. February. March. April. May. June. July. August. September. October. November. December.

Sunday. Monday. Tuesday. Wednesday. Thursday. Friday. Saturday

01|02|03|04|05|06|07|08|09|10|11|12|13|14|15|16|17|18|19|20|21|22|23|24|25|26|27|28|29|30

January. February. March. April. May. June. July. August. September. October. November. December.

Sunday. Monday. Tuesday. Wednesday. Thursday. Friday. Saturday

01|02|03|04|05|06|07|08|09|10|11|12|13|14|15|16|17|18|19|20|21|22|23|24|25|26|27|28|29|30

January. February. March. April. May. June. July. August. September. October. November. December.

Sunday. Monday. Tuesday. Wednesday. Thursday. Friday. Saturday

01|02|03|04|05|06|07|08|09|10|11|12|13|14|15|16|17|18|19|20|21|22|23|24|25|26|27|28|29|30

January. February. March. April. May. June. July. August. September. October. November. December.

Sunday. Monday. Tuesday. Wednesday. Thursday. Friday. Saturday

01|02|03|04|05|06|07|08|09|10|11|12|13|14|15|16|17|18|19|20|21|22|23|24|25|26|27|28|29|30

January. February. March. April. May. June. July. August. September. October. November. December.

Sunday. Monday. Tuesday. Wednesday. Thursday. Friday. Saturday

01|02|03|04|05|06|07|08|09|10|11|12|13|14|15|16|17|18|19|20|21|22|23|24|25|26|27|28|29|30

....

....

....

....

....

....

....

....

....

....

....

....

....

....

....

....

....

....

....

....

....

....

....

....

....

....

....

....

....

....

January. February. March. April. May. June. July. August. September. October. November. December.

Sunday. Monday. Tuesday. Wednesday. Thursday. Friday. Saturday

01|02|03|04|05|06|07|08|09|10|11|12|13|14|15|16|17|18|19|20|21|22|23|24|25|26|27|28|29|30

....
....
....
....
....
....
....
....
....
....
....
....
....
....
....
....
....
....
....
....
....
....
....
....
....
....
....
....
....
....
....
....

January. February. March. April. May. June. July. August. September. October. November. December.

Sunday. Monday. Tuesday. Wednesday. Thursday. Friday. Saturday

01|02|03|04|05|06|07|08|09|10|11|12|13|14|15|16|17|18|19|20|21|22|23|24|25|26|27|28|29|30

....
....
....
....
....
....
....
....
....
....
....
....
....
....
....
....
....
....
....
....
....
....
....
....
....
....
....
....
....
....

January. February. March. April. May. June. July. August. September. October. November. December.

Sunday. Monday. Tuesday. Wednesday. Thursday. Friday. Saturday

01|02|03|04|05|06|07|08|09|10|11|12|13|14|15|16|17|18|19|20|21|22|23|24|25|26|27|28|29|30

January. February. March. April. May. June. July. August. September. October. November. December.

Sunday. Monday. Tuesday. Wednesday. Thursday. Friday. Saturday

01|02|03|04|05|06|07|08|09|10|11|12|13|14|15|16|17|18|19|20|21|22|23|24|25|26|27|28|29|30

....

....

....

....

....

....

....

....

....

....

....

....

....

....

....

....

....

....

....

....

....

....

....

....

....

....

....

....

....

....

January. February. March. April. May. June. July. August. September. October. November. December.

Sunday. Monday. Tuesday. Wednesday. Thursday. Friday. Saturday

01|02|03|04|05|06|07|08|09|10|11|12|13|14|15|16|17|18|19|20|21|22|23|24|25|26|27|28|29|30

January. February. March. April. May. June. July. August. September. October. November. December.

Sunday. Monday. Tuesday. Wednesday. Thursday. Friday. Saturday

01|02|03|04|05|06|07|08|09|10|11|12|13|14|15|16|17|18|19|20|21|22|23|24|25|26|27|28|29|30

January. February. March. April. May. June. July. August. September. October. November. December.

Sunday. Monday. Tuesday. Wednesday. Thursday. Friday. Saturday

01|02|03|04|05|06|07|08|09|10|11|12|13|14|15|16|17|18|19|20|21|22|23|24|25|26|27|28|29|30

January. February. March. April. May. June. July. August. September. October. November. December.

Sunday. Monday. Tuesday. Wednesday. Thursday. Friday. Saturday

01|02|03|04|05|06|07|08|09|10|11|12|13|14|15|16|17|18|19|20|21|22|23|24|25|26|27|28|29|30

January. February. March. April. May. June. July. August. September. October. November. December.

Sunday. Monday. Tuesday. Wednesday. Thursday. Friday. Saturday

01|02|03|04|05|06|07|08|09|10|11|12|13|14|15|16|17|18|19|20|21|22|23|24|25|26|27|28|29|30

January. February. March. April. May. June. July. August. September. October. November. December.

Sunday. Monday. Tuesday. Wednesday. Thursday. Friday. Saturday

01|02|03|04|05|06|07|08|09|10|11|12|13|14|15|16|17|18|19|20|21|22|23|24|25|26|27|28|29|30

....
....
....
....
....
....
....
....
....
....
....
....
....
....
....
....
....
....
....
....
....
....
....
....
....
....
....
....
....
....

January.February.March.April.May.June.July.August.September.October.November.December.

Sunday.Monday.Tuesday.Wednesday.Thursday.Friday.Saturday

01|02|03|04|05|06|07|08|09|10|11|12|13|14|15|16|17|18|19|20|21|22|23|24|25|26|27|28|29|30

January.February.March.April.May.June.July.August.September.October.November.December.

Sunday.Monday.Tuesday.Wednesday.Thursday.Friday.Saturday

01|02|03|04|05|06|07|08|09|10|11|12|13|14|15|16|17|18|19|20|21|22|23|24|25|26|27|28|29|30

....

....

....

....

....

....

....

....

....

....

....

....

....

....

....

....

....

....

....

....

....

....

....

....

....

....

....

....

....

....

January. February. March. April. May. June. July. August. September. October. November. December.

Sunday. Monday. Tuesday. Wednesday. Thursday. Friday. Saturday

01|02|03|04|05|06|07|08|09|10|11|12|13|14|15|16|17|18|19|20|21|22|23|24|25|26|27|28|29|30

January. February. March. April. May. June. July. August. September. October. November. December.

Sunday. Monday. Tuesday. Wednesday. Thursday. Friday. Saturday

01|02|03|04|05|06|07|08|09|10|11|12|13|14|15|16|17|18|19|20|21|22|23|24|25|26|27|28|29|30

....
....
....
....
....
....
....
....
....
....
....
....
....
....
....
....
....
....
....
....
....
....
....
....
....
....
....
....
....
....
....

January. February. March. April. May. June. July. August. September. October. November. December.

Sunday. Monday. Tuesday. Wednesday. Thursday. Friday. Saturday

01|02|03|04|05|06|07|08|09|10|11|12|13|14|15|16|17|18|19|20|21|22|23|24|25|26|27|28|29|30

January. February. March. April. May. June. July. August. September. October. November. December.

Sunday. Monday. Tuesday. Wednesday. Thursday. Friday. Saturday

01|02|03|04|05|06|07|08|09|10|11|12|13|14|15|16|17|18|19|20|21|22|23|24|25|26|27|28|29|30

....
....
....
....
....
....
....
....
....
....
....
....
....
....
....
....
....
....
....
....
....
....
....
....
....
....
....
....
....
....

January. February. March. April. May. June. July. August. September. October. November. December.

Sunday. Monday. Tuesday. Wednesday. Thursday. Friday. Saturday

01|02|03|04|05|06|07|08|09|10|11|12|13|14|15|16|17|18|19|20|21|22|23|24|25|26|27|28|29|30

January. February. March. April. May. June. July. August. September. October. November. December.

Sunday. Monday. Tuesday. Wednesday. Thursday. Friday. Saturday

01|02|03|04|05|06|07|08|09|10|11|12|13|14|15|16|17|18|19|20|21|22|23|24|25|26|27|28|29|30

January. February. March. April. May. June. July. August. September. October. November. December.

Sunday. Monday. Tuesday. Wednesday. Thursday. Friday. Saturday

01|02|03|04|05|06|07|08|09|10|11|12|13|14|15|16|17|18|19|20|21|22|23|24|25|26|27|28|29|30

January. February. March. April. May. June. July. August. September. October. November. December.

Sunday. Monday. Tuesday. Wednesday. Thursday. Friday. Saturday

01|02|03|04|05|06|07|08|09|10|11|12|13|14|15|16|17|18|19|20|21|22|23|24|25|26|27|28|29|30

January. February. March. April. May. June. July. August. September. October. November. December.

Sunday. Monday. Tuesday. Wednesday. Thursday. Friday. Saturday

01|02|03|04|05|06|07|08|09|10|11|12|13|14|15|16|17|18|19|20|21|22|23|24|25|26|27|28|29|30

January.February.March.April.May.June.July.August.September.October.November.December.

Sunday.Monday.Tuesday.Wednesday.Thursday.Friday.Saturday

01|02|03|04|05|06|07|08|09|10|11|12|13|14|15|16|17|18|19|20|21|22|23|24|25|26|27|28|29|30

348

January. February. March. April. May. June. July. August. September. October. November. December.

Sunday. Monday. Tuesday. Wednesday. Thursday. Friday. Saturday

01|02|03|04|05|06|07|08|09|10|11|12|13|14|15|16|17|18|19|20|21|22|23|24|25|26|27|28|29|30

January. February. March. April. May. June. July. August. September. October. November. December.

Sunday. Monday. Tuesday. Wednesday. Thursday. Friday. Saturday

01|02|03|04|05|06|07|08|09|10|11|12|13|14|15|16|17|18|19|20|21|22|23|24|25|26|27|28|29|30

....

....

....

....

....

....

....

....

....

....

....

....

....

....

....

....

....

....

....

....

....

....

....

....

....

....

....

....

....

....

....

....

January. February. March. April. May. June. July. August. September. October. November. December.

Sunday. Monday. Tuesday. Wednesday. Thursday. Friday. Saturday

01|02|03|04|05|06|07|08|09|10|11|12|13|14|15|16|17|18|19|20|21|22|23|24|25|26|27|28|29|30

January. February. March. April. May. June. July. August. September. October. November. December.

Sunday. Monday. Tuesday. Wednesday. Thursday. Friday. Saturday

01|02|03|04|05|06|07|08|09|10|11|12|13|14|15|16|17|18|19|20|21|22|23|24|25|26|27|28|29|30

....
....
....
....
....
....
....
....
....
....
....
....
....
....
....
....
....
....
....
....
....
....
....
....
....
....
....
....
....
....

January. February. March. April. May. June. July. August. September. October. November. December.

Sunday. Monday. Tuesday. Wednesday. Thursday. Friday. Saturday

01|02|03|04|05|06|07|08|09|10|11|12|13|14|15|16|17|18|19|20|21|22|23|24|25|26|27|28|29|30

January. February. March. April. May. June. July. August. September. October. November. December.

Sunday. Monday. Tuesday. Wednesday. Thursday. Friday. Saturday

01|02|03|04|05|06|07|08|09|10|11|12|13|14|15|16|17|18|19|20|21|22|23|24|25|26|27|28|29|30

January. February. March. April. May. June. July. August. September. October. November. December.

Sunday. Monday. Tuesday. Wednesday. Thursday. Friday. Saturday

01|02|03|04|05|06|07|08|09|10|11|12|13|14|15|16|17|18|19|20|21|22|23|24|25|26|27|28|29|30

January. February. March. April. May. June. July. August. September. October. November. December.

Sunday. Monday. Tuesday. Wednesday. Thursday. Friday. Saturday

01|02|03|04|05|06|07|08|09|10|11|12|13|14|15|16|17|18|19|20|21|22|23|24|25|26|27|28|29|30

January. February. March. April. May. June. July. August. September. October. November. December.

Sunday. Monday. Tuesday. Wednesday. Thursday. Friday. Saturday

01|02|03|04|05|06|07|08|09|10|11|12|13|14|15|16|17|18|19|20|21|22|23|24|25|26|27|28|29|30

January. February. March. April. May. June. July. August. September. October. November. December.

Sunday. Monday. Tuesday. Wednesday. Thursday. Friday. Saturday

01|02|03|04|05|06|07|08|09|10|11|12|13|14|15|16|17|18|19|20|21|22|23|24|25|26|27|28|29|30

....

....

....

....

....

....

....

....

....

....

....

....

....

....

....

....

....

....

....

....

....

....

....

....

....

....

....

....

....

....

....

....

....

January. February. March. April. May. June. July. August. September. October. November. December.

Sunday. Monday. Tuesday. Wednesday. Thursday. Friday. Saturday

01|02|03|04|05|06|07|08|09|10|11|12|13|14|15|16|17|18|19|20|21|22|23|24|25|26|27|28|29|30

January. February. March. April. May. June. July. August. September. October. November. December.

Sunday. Monday. Tuesday. Wednesday. Thursday. Friday. Saturday

01|02|03|04|05|06|07|08|09|10|11|12|13|14|15|16|17|18|19|20|21|22|23|24|25|26|27|28|29|30

January. February. March. April. May. June. July. August. September. October. November. December.

Sunday. Monday. Tuesday. Wednesday. Thursday. Friday. Saturday

01|02|03|04|05|06|07|08|09|10|11|12|13|14|15|16|17|18|19|20|21|22|23|24|25|26|27|28|29|30

January. February. March. April. May. June. July. August. September. October. November. December.

Sunday. Monday. Tuesday. Wednesday. Thursday. Friday. Saturday

01|02|03|04|05|06|07|08|09|10|11|12|13|14|15|16|17|18|19|20|21|22|23|24|25|26|27|28|29|30

January. February. March. April. May. June. July. August. September. October. November. December.

Sunday. Monday. Tuesday. Wednesday. Thursday. Friday. Saturday

01|02|03|04|05|06|07|08|09|10|11|12|13|14|15|16|17|18|19|20|21|22|23|24|25|26|27|28|29|30

January. February. March. April. May. June. July. August. September. October. November. December.

Sunday. Monday. Tuesday. Wednesday. Thursday. Friday. Saturday

01|02|03|04|05|06|07|08|09|10|11|12|13|14|15|16|17|18|19|20|21|22|23|24|25|26|27|28|29|30

....
....
....
....
....
....
....
....
....
....
....
....
....
....
....
....
....
....
....
....
....
....
....
....
....
....
....
....
....
....

January.February.March.April.May.June.July.August.September.October.November.December.

Sunday.Monday.Tuesday.Wednesday.Thursday.Friday.Saturday

01|02|03|04|05|06|07|08|09|10|11|12|13|14|15|16|17|18|19|20|21|22|23|24|25|26|27|28|29|30

....
....
....
....
....
....
....
....
....
....
....
....
....
....
....
....
....
....
....
....
....
....
....
....
....
....
....
....
....
....
....
....

January. February. March. April. May. June. July. August. September. October. November. December.

Sunday. Monday. Tuesday. Wednesday. Thursday. Friday. Saturday

01|02|03|04|05|06|07|08|09|10|11|12|13|14|15|16|17|18|19|20|21|22|23|24|25|26|27|28|29|30

....
....
....
....
....
....
....
....
....
....
....
....
....
....
....
....
....
....
....
....
....
....
....
....
....
....
....
....
....
....
....
....

January. February. March. April. May. June. July. August. September. October. November. December.

Sunday. Monday. Tuesday. Wednesday. Thursday. Friday. Saturday

01|02|03|04|05|06|07|08|09|10|11|12|13|14|15|16|17|18|19|20|21|22|23|24|25|26|27|28|29|30

....
....
....
....
....
....
....
....
....
....
....
....
....
....
....
....
....
....
....
....
....
....
....
....
....
....
....
....
....
....

January. February. March. April. May. June. July. August. September. October. November. December.

Sunday. Monday. Tuesday. Wednesday. Thursday. Friday. Saturday

01|02|03|04|05|06|07|08|09|10|11|12|13|14|15|16|17|18|19|20|21|22|23|24|25|26|27|28|29|30

....

....

....

....

....

....

....

....

....

....

....

....

....

....

....

....

....

....

....

....

....

....

....

....

....

....

....

....

January. February. March. April. May. June. July. August. September. October. November. December.

Sunday. Monday. Tuesday. Wednesday. Thursday. Friday. Saturday

01|02|03|04|05|06|07|08|09|10|11|12|13|14|15|16|17|18|19|20|21|22|23|24|25|26|27|28|29|30

....
....
....
....
....
....
....
....
....
....
....
....
....
....
....
....
....
....
....
....
....
....
....
....
....
....
....
....
....
....
....

January. February. March. April. May. June. July. August. September. October. November. December.

Sunday. Monday. Tuesday. Wednesday. Thursday. Friday. Saturday

01|02|03|04|05|06|07|08|09|10|11|12|13|14|15|16|17|18|19|20|21|22|23|24|25|26|27|28|29|30

....

....

....

....

....

....

....

....

....

....

....

....

....

....

....

....

....

....

....

....

....

....

....

....

....

....

....

....

....

....

....

....